Drifting in and out

of my Two Worlds

Jessica Thorpe

The dedication of this book goes out three ways: To each and every Selective Mutism sufferer out there, misunderstood and suffering in silence, to all of the parents and people involved with selectively mute children, and to all my friends and family who know who they are.

Foreword:

This book has primarily been written, above all, for parents who wish to experience for themselves what life is like for their children living with Selective Mutism from a sufferer's point of view. In depth, as parents and sufferers alike have said before concerning the first edition of the autobiography, it covers how children and older sufferers feel in anxiety provoking situations, what they are thinking, many of the symptoms they may exhibit, and a general picture of what life is like when you have an actual fear of speaking. There are limited resources around for Selective Mutism and much of what one hears is from text book descriptions, but this story reflects exactly what it is like when living with this harrowing anxiety disorder. I would like to promote awareness so more children and sufferers can be helped and therefore treated sooner before the mutism becomes too entrenched and then more challenging to treat. My brother and I have suffered with Selective Mutism for most of our lives but I, miraculously, overcome it on my own accord without any external help.

This autobiography explicates in depth my experiences growing up with this condition. I share my experiences living with Selective Mutism, putting across how it feels to have it, and courses of action which contributed to helping me overcome it in the latter chapters. The best way to describe having Selective Mutism would be to say that it feels as though your throat is physically paralysed or physically closing up. When you think about it, speaking is just as simple as speaking - if you can't do it, you just push yourself and speak anyway. But it isn't really like that. You cannot speak any more than you can be convinced not to feel pain during an injury. To somebody with no knowledge of the condition, it can evidently be very difficult to understand. This is why the intention of this book is to put out there how it really is to suffer with a paralysing fear of speaking. Having examined my mental processes and behaviour through introspection both influenced by my Selective Mutism during all of which time I suffered with it, I managed to gain an extensive understanding of the condition itself. I would therefore like to spend my life helping others with their Selective Mutism and conducting further studies into it so we can shed more light into this dreadful disorder.

Would you demand a deaf child to listen? So why must a Selective Mutism sufferer be forced to speak?

Introduction – *What is Selective Mutism?* –

There I silently sat at the back corner of my year eleven religious education class drowning in isolation. The unwelcome taste of apprehension tightly clutched the back of my throat as I sat eagerly awaiting the approach of the end of the lesson.

"Oi, Mute!" Emily called coolly from two desks in front of me. Reluctantly, I looked up at her.

"Why don't you ever speak?" *Why does it bother you why I never speak?* Is what I wanted to call back. Only I couldn't. The words were there, but buried deep, stuck in my throat like a dry bone, and no matter how hard I tried to pull them out, it still felt like nothing more than a paralysis to the throat. The back of my throat was so dry it hurt. In disregard to Emily's question, I sat there staring down onto the face of my desk in my world of introspective thought. Her eyes, dull, seemingly from lack of sleep, remained on me. Eye contact was threatening to me.

"Come on, why don't you ever speak?" I began to question why she continued when she knew I wouldn't answer; needless to say she was just testing her luck by means of her attempts to try and get me to speak as the others had always

1

done. I repressed the urge to ignore her. Instead, I shrugged my shoulders in a timid gesture as I usually did in regard to a question at school. Meanwhile, Kane, beside whom I sat, watched thoughtfully and grinned at the absurdity of this one way conversation.

"Seriously, why *don't* you ever speak though? Have you got a really deep voice that you don't like? Or … or are you scared that -" his face suddenly lit up as if he had just been given an electric shock, "- is it because you have *braces?*" Braces? Just when I thought I had heard it all … it was almost as foolish as the last assumption another student had made, "Are you on a really long sponsored silence?" For a moment I imagined such a thing. I failed to understand why anybody in the world would feel the need to be that charitable … Kane shrugged his shoulders in a way as if to mimic my last gesture. A long heavy sigh escaped his chapped, weather-cracked lips.

"Is that all you can do!" he said rather more rhetorically than implying a question. In a sense, yes, that was all I could do in such instances. Kane was a confident and socially outgoing boy who had a reputation for being the class clown. He was well-built with warm, grey hair formed into a ruffled array of what they considered to be style and wore thick glasses which seemed to magnify his eyes to double their original size. Despite his efforts, he was beginning to lack patience.

"TALK, MAN!" I ignored him. I glanced out of the window from nerves at the grey sky which appeared to pose an imminent threat of rain. The sun was struggling hard to break through the clouds.

"Leave Mute alone, Kane. She doesn't like you. Why *else* do you think she isn't speaking to you?" Emily called to him again whilst fiddling with her pen in a dreary manner. It had seemed Kane's now one way conversation had interrupted her day dream.

"You don't like me?" he asked sounding half ashamed, half amused. I ignored him, feeling self-pity being unable to speak. I looked back down onto the work at the desk in front of me, *The Five Pillars of Islam*. I didn't have a clue of what to write. Religious education, I was content with the knowledge that it always was my least of all favourite of subjects after mathematics. It didn't get much worse than mathematics …

"SPEAK!" Kane demanded impatiently. The two Turkish girls at the desk in front of us, behind Emily, turned in slight alarm. Zelia and Kaya looked me up and down for several moments as if I were totally inferior when compared to themselves. I twiddled the ends of my hair into my mouth.

"Do you fancy her?" Zelia asked him suspiciously.

"*NO!* She's just a mate!" he said almost automatically. Lie. Nobody would sit next to *me* in class unless they fancied me. I sat at the back of all of my classes, preferably by the window where I was rarely seen and never heard. It was always an odd benefit if the window beside me stood slightly ajar so a cool spring breeze could caress my cheeks; but I dare not ever open the window myself. Acting non-verbally was always just as nerve-wrenching as acting verbally.

"Just a good ol' mate, ain't ya'?" I forced a smile.

"Kaya, have you ever heard this girl speak before?" Zelia inquired her friend. By now, my whole row was listening in to them. Their work lay forgotten amid the many scattered papers on their desks.

"She can't. She hasn't spoken once in the entire five years that she's been in our classes … since year seven." They exchanged shocked looks.

"Oh my God, why doesn't she speak?" Zelia asked rather irritatingly.

"She doesn't have a voice box." Kaya added.

"*Don't* you?"

"Stop asking her stupid questions, look at how nervous she is!" Kane snapped apparently a lot louder than he had seemingly initially intended to. That was a knife through the heart. The class fell silent and our teacher, Mr Scollard, looked at me attentively from his desk at the front of the class. At that moment, a cold heavy rain began to beat against the window as the wind emitted a steady drone, almost as if my feelings could manipulate the weather. My throat closed even tighter and my heart drummed even harder against my ribs. The nerve-shredding tensions … The interactive whiteboard which reside at the front of the class seemed a good point to focus on. I stared at it as if fascinated by it despite hardly acknowledging its presence. I began to breathe faster. I felt another panic attack coming on. There was for some reason, a long, uncomfortable, silence, and then the whole class turned to look at me leaving me feeling fairly fazed. The anxiety was tearing me to shreds as the knot in my stomach was twisting.

"Guys, what seems to be the problem here?" Mr Scollard asked calmly. Mr Scollard was very tall and had an old fashioned dress sense along with long dread locks which he often kept tied behind him. Mr Scollard was a patient, well-meaning teacher. It was seldom to hear him raise his voice within the classroom. Kane then spoke again, "As I was just saying, sir, these two here keep on looking at her and they're making her feel nervous." There was a long pause perturbed by the rain dancing on the roof.

"Is this true, girls?" Mr Scollard asked.

"No! We were just wondering why she never speaks!" Zelia debated. Mr Scollard's eyes then fell back upon me, observing me in the most scrutinising of ways as if he was waiting for me to retaliate Zelia's point, but perhaps something in my expression told him differently because then he said, "OK guys, get back on with your work, please ..." Most heads turned back round. I once again felt like a total misfit. *Thanks for that, Kane!* As always, the only thing I felt like doing was being swallowed up by the ground. The rain slid silver down the glass of the window beside me.

"I can also tell you're nervous because of the way you're sliding the lid on and off of your pen so quickly," Kane mumbled in an undertone. The terror did not end. I breathed a deep sigh. Who was he? A psychiatrist? And of that matter, I cast my eyes down at my hand. So I was. How long had I been doing that for? I smiled as I always did. Smiling, it was almost like an inhibition - something that I did almost without being able to control in most instances. Still, it seemed the only way I could show my appreciation. I looked behind at the clock for perhaps the fifth time that lesson. Fifty minutes of it had expired. It had seemed like an eternity. My throat still ached yet another miserable few hours of it still lie ahead. I couldn't wait until after school. It was the only thing which kept me going throughout, what was for me, the long, miserable school day. In the meantime, Kane was still working on the great accomplishment of trying to somehow trick me into speaking.

"Is he getting on your nerves?" Emily called, x-raying my thoughts. I gave a feeble nod.

"Do you want me to stop speaking to you now?" Kane then asked. I nodded enthusiastically this time.

"OK. I'll try."

Later that day after school had long finished, the sun had broken through the clouds and beamed upon the people about the park, striking at them like arrows. No more clouds cluttered the sky and afternoon shadows stretched long and thin. The park was surrounded by houses and flats of some of the people who came to the park. Among some of these people, were a large group of boys playing football, with a girl. The girl, in a bossy demeanour, was shouting assertively and encouraging her team-mates enthusiastically. Not a minute went by without the girl yelling her motivation at everybody with the loudest voice she could muster. Her shouts echoed through the park while her team mate dribbled the ball towards the opposing goal, sprinting determinedly with legs on fire.

"LOOK UP, ALL THE WAY – DON'T STOP..." Her team mate struck, yet missed.

"ARGHH! UNLUCKY, LITTLE MAN!" the girl shouted with further enthusiasm down the pitch. The girl had always had a passion for football. When she played, her body sizzled with euphoria and confidence whilst she forgot the negative aspects of her multidimensional life. Football was the sport to play when she needed to let out the bitterness she felt inside. The girl was bossy and loved to be heard. She was too much of a normal girl living a normal life, nothing could have brought to light any indication of her other world. Just then, she won the ball, tearing down the pitch at high pace tasting the sharpness of competition in the air and powered it into the top left corner of the goal whilst the trees around her danced gracefully in the light wind. She celebrated confidently,

running like the wind with her arms outstretched like the winner of a marathon, yelling her cheers beneath the vast skies aflame with the setting sun as the sunlight slipped through her fingers.
"WHAT A GOAL, *JESS!*"
The girl was me.

Selective Mutism is a complex, childhood, anxiety disorder in which sufferers are unable to speak and communicate effectively in select social settings or situations given severe anxiety. Selectively mutes are fully capable of understanding language and are able to speak in places where they feel comfortable and relaxed, particularly at home with immediate family members. Many are mute at school for years while at home or in select other environments are extremely talkative. They have an actual fear of speaking and of social actions when and where there is an expectation to speak. Sufferers avoid their anxiety by not speaking. When the sufferer senses an expectation to speak, they are faced with great difficulty initiating conversation or responding in a verbal manner. Ninety per cent of these individuals also suffer from social anxiety or social phobia.

On the negative side, selectively mutes find it difficult to maintain eye contact. They do not often smile and display blank facial expressions. They find situations where talking is normally expected very frightening and difficult to handle. Excessive worrying and fears are also very common symptoms found in selectively mutes. If left untreated, Selective Mutism can potentially lead to much greater serious problems in later life, such as depression, social isolation, underachievement in school and the work place, binge drinking, eating disorders, and even suicide. In order for the child to have met the criteria for Selective Mutism, the mutism must have persisted for at least one month followed by the child being unable to speak in 'select' social settings such as school or other social places. While content in a comfortable environment, most selectively mute children are as normal as any other child.

Although it is debatable, Selective Mutism is rare, roughly affecting six children in every one thousand. The incidence of this disorder is slightly higher in girls than boys and usually starts at nursery or at the beginning of school when children are outside of their family.

There are many contributing factors which are believed to be of cause to Selective Mutism. A number of selectively mutes have a genetic predisposition to anxiety. They have inherited the tendency from various family members which may make them vulnerable to the development of an anxiety disorder. Significant life events that may have occurred of change or loss may also be cause to the mutism. A stressful environment could also be the risk factor, and as well as a history of migration, there is a prevalence in bilingual ethnic-minority families. I would like to strongly emphasise, however, that Selective Mutism is *not* caused by abuse, neglect or trauma. This assumption is believed widely today and there have been numerous cases where Social Services have been involved and have refused to consider the diagnosis for Selective Mutism.

Some of the signs of anxiety that children with Selective Mutism display include: Separating from parents, clinging behaviour, disobedience, easily frustrated, inflexibility/stubbornness, sleep problems, frequent tantrums, distractibility, playing alone or not playing at all, difficulty completing tasks, crying easily, trichotillomania (skin picking, hair pulling), and extreme shyness from infancy onwards.

Behavioural manifestations at home commonly include: Moodiness, procrastination, temper tantrums, need for control, bossiness, domination and extreme talkativeness.

On the other hand, selectively mutes display positive tendencies and symptoms such as: A high level of introspectiveness (in which they are able to demonstrate a better understanding of the world around them than that of peers of their own age), above average perception, inquisitiveness and intelligence, creativity, and they generally appear to show sensitivity towards other's thoughts, feelings and empathy. A number of these sufferers are born with inhibited temperaments meaning they are more likely to be fearful and wary of new people or situations. They have a decreased threshold of excitability in the part of the brain called the amygdala. The function of the amygdala is to receive and process signs of potential danger and to set off a series of reactions which will help the individual protect themselves. In anxious individuals, the amygdala over reacts and sets off these responses when the individual isn't in danger; it sets off the fight-or-flight response within a person. Sufferers with Selective Mutism have their speech shut down whenever they enter a situation where there is an expectation to speak.

Selectively mutes will often stand motionless and expressionless, turn their heads in the opposite direction, and sometimes demonstrate awkward and stiff body language. Further, they can also be very sensitive to noise and crowds and have great difficulty when talking about and expressing their own feelings. Many selectively mute children, too, develop Sensory Integration Disorder. They may display symptoms such as showing sensitivity towards touch, sound, and movement. Some sufferers do cope and participate in school by performing non-verbally and talking to a select few. Some children, on the other hand, may appear outwardly calm and communicate only when they are asked a question, never initiating conversation. These are the children who are usually overlooked and misinterpreted as being defiant or oppositional since they do not show visible signs of being nervous. What is more, most tend to have difficulty initiating (starting a conversation), and may be slow to respond even when it comes to non-verbal communication. This can lead to a misinterpretation of their cognitive ability and be of great frustration to them.

Unfortunately, information, resources and research studies on Selective Mutism are scarce and in a lot of cases, professionals have not been taught anything at all about Selective Mutism. They are often given inaccurate and misleading information, and as a result, doctors, teachers and other professionals will say a child is slow to warm up or just shy and will outgrow their behaviour. Other professionals incorrectly interpret Selective Mutism as, in a lot of instances, Autism, oppositional or defiant behaviour where the mutism is a means of manipulating and controlling other people. For the true selectively mutes, these views are wrong and only exacerbate the case resulting in mutism more entrenched. As I was soon to discover, an entire school career in the absence of any diagnosis whatsoever would prove to be traumatic …

Chapter One – Selective Mutism and I –

My life began on the fifth of June, 1992, in Enfield, London, situated in the United Kingdom and I was named Jessica Zara Thorpe inheriting my father's surname of English ancestry, and to unmarried parents. My home town, Enfield, was ten miles North of London and was first recorded in 1086 as Enefelde where I moved into my very first home. We lived on the second storey of three unaccustomed flats down a quiet road of the outer suburbs with nothing but the red tint of the bricks and the lush vegetation of the grass to liven the outlook. I lived in a quiet, well-off neighbourhood a few roads down from the shops and the main road.

In virtue of my father, he was of average height with feathers of ash brown hair and deep-set, green eyes. He was at the best of times, a respectably friendly, boisterous, vivacious man with rather an appreciative sense of humour. At other times, he could be selfish, ignorant, and very careless. It is impossible not to be struck with the fact that he was very dependent on alcohol. I have a dim recollection of him returning home from work every night, as a builder, blind drunk, after he would casually hit the bottle at the pub since he too had been raised by a family who frequently abused alcohol. He was a heavy gambler, too. My father and I got along rather well. Straining my memory, he was, at the best of times, a laugh to have around. He was one who expressed the *live fast, and die young* attitude, if you like. I cannot say I considered him in a fatherly way. He gave me his attention, but it was my mother who always put me before everything else. When my mother had once suggested buying me toys, his response was, "What does she need toys for? You only end up throwing them away in a few years time. Waste of money."

My mother, nonetheless, was quite the opposite. Her warm brown hair fell down along her pale face next to her soulful blue eyes. When I was born, she had not long celebrated her twenty eighth birthday. She was quite active and in her days and used to race for the borough. She stopped working in time for my birth, always tried her very best for me and always spent all of her time with me bringing me up the in the best ways that she could. She brought me up in a disciplined, easy manner and had given me as much freedom as I would have been fond of having. She pretty much let me do whatever I wanted and go where I wanted, whenever I wanted. As far as I am concerned, she had provided me with a reasonable atmosphere to be brought up in.

As a matter of course, I believe my Selective Mutism was likely to be comprised of a combination of contributing factors opposed to one single cause. All things considered, I had come to think that my predisposition to anxiety had played quite a reasonable part in my Selective Mutism. A strong family history of anxiety was often present in selectively mutes and I had assumed I had inherited mine from my mother since she had appeared to show the notable signs of anxiety at given times. Combined with another notable factor, stressors and a somewhat psychological trauma during the time of my speech development, may also have encouraged the Selective Mutism. By cause of this, since my father had been an alcoholic, there had often been a lot of heavy shouting, arguing, and fighting going on during the time when I had just started to develop socially, emotionally and intellectually. Thus, environmental stressors may also have played a small significance in which too much attention was provoked onto me from other people for not speaking, exacerbated further by misunderstandings of my parents and, in due course, teachers, believing I would grow out of my mutism. I believe these environmental stressors which exacerbate the mutism are reflected in numerous other cases of sufferers with Selective Mutism.

Since my mother naturally grew fed up with my father's alcohol abuse, we moved temporarily into a house leaving him behind where I celebrated my very first birthday. I felt I had been better off here at the time. We had had good neighbours with daughters my age who came over to keep me company and our next door neighbour's cat came to our house which pleased me. Despite our departure from the first flat, my father's family came along to the party and he must have made another promise that he would stop drinking because, after that, we moved back into our flat a month to the latter. To my yearning delight, if he hadn't been doing so surreptitiously which I doubt, anyhow, he seemed to have put the bottle back down for a while after that.

I believe the first signs of my Selective Mutism initiated at the age of around six months. I was very withdrawn and displayed a blank, frozen, look on my face, and my body language came across very motionless. At a later age of one, my mother proceeded in taking me to Play Group. At such age, it seemed I had no interest in my fellow peers since the only social interactions I ever engaged in were seldom looking at other babies to see what they were doing. I rarely smiled and never made a sound with my tiny shrill of a voice. Other babies laughed, cried, shouted, or made some kind of monosyllabic babbling noise - but not me. I'm not convinced I even took into consideration that I had a voice by reason that I felt so comfortable not speaking or interacting. Of course, people just labelled me as a *'shy'* baby.

To the best of my remembrance, I can recall small episodes at the Christmas party at play group. I can vividly remember biting off every sugar paper decoration upon the mountain of cupcakes piled up beneath a plate on the food table before me (since they seemed to be the only thing I would eat) whilst I watched the other kids stuff their faces senselessly with the foods I was too stubborn to try. Further, I spoke my first words at a normal age of around nine months and my first word was 'cat' followed by my second word, 'Mum.' I had had tons upon tons of Teddy bears throughout my childhood and my favourite had been a cat soft toy which I got from the playgroup at Christmas which meowed when its belly was pressed, hence my first word. I would refuse to leave home without my Teddies, I was very clingy over them. Contrary to the majority of babies, however, I did not approve of dummies. I would always spit them back out and had just seen them as a plug to stop babies from crying and so had never worn one.

From the age of three, I took little pleasure in attending a toddler group close to home. I dreaded it. For a considerable amount of time, I never smiled nor uttered a word. I was completely mute around almost everybody in my life apart from my parents and my grandmother from my mother's side of the family. My mother was with me at all times and spoke for me on every occasion. She was my voice. Seemingly, this was why I suffered severely with separation anxiety. I was securely attached. Every morning, it was a mission for her to drop me off because it felt to me as if a big part of me had been snatched away when she was gone - my voice. I cried hysterically when she tried to leave me. I detested being around unfamiliar people and felt ridiculously stubborn. I cannot even stress the severity of my attachment. Equally, it felt as if it had been illegal for me to speak because it came as such an impossible task to me. I had quite simply learned to avoid my anxiety by not attempting to speak. Incredible amounts of anxiety would rush through me when I was asked a direct question, particularly by an unfamiliar person; my throat would feel as if it was physically closing up, and because it was so difficult to pull the words out, I had convinced myself I didn't even *want* to speak. My mother and some peers had to occupy me with some toys whilst I battled with the palpitating beats of my heart, and the next time I turned, my mother would be running towards the exit doors. At the worst of times, people had to pull me off of her. Nevertheless, I was fortunate enough to have made a few friends who I was able to speak with spontaneously while we were out of the way on our own. My two closest friends were Nicole and Louise who I had met through playgroup. Nicole had blonde hair and blue eyes, like myself, and shared my age. Louise, however, had chestnut, mahogany brown hair, brown eyes, freckles, and was around a year younger than I.

As the days ensued, my mother soon met Louise's mother, Tracy, and we soon began seeing them on a regular basis. Tracy was a friendly, humorous, and motherly individual who was a great role model to all. She had long, ginger hair and pretty facial features. Eventually, given the absence of Toddler Group, I before long began to speak to Tracy and Louise very loquaciously. During the summer on hot days, my mother and I would go over to their house and Louise and I would paddle in the bubble-bath shrouded pool, splashing about blissfully wearing our Minnie Mouse swimming costumes in her back garden. When lunch time struck, we would go down to the chip shop and then come back to Tracy's and eat at the table in the most spectacular garden. Beauty flew from all corners of it and I had never before known so many different flowers. My favourite was the snap-dragon flower: the flower which opened and closed its mouth when laterally squeezed which we referred to as the rabbit flower. Sometimes, Louise would pick me one from her garden to give to me before Play Group. After that, we would devour scrumptious slices of Battenberg cake before the peace was then disturbed when we got out the plastic tennis rackets, and after batting the balls over the fences, we would acquire the plastic fruit from her play house until that had all been temporarily batted over the fences too. We would then go into the playhouse and play 'Doctors and Nurses' or 'Mummies and Daddies' with the toys Louise had. Then, after a while of playing games, I would, feeling very reluctant, go home with my mother. From time to time, we often went on outings with Tracy and Louise to which I thoroughly enjoyed: to amusement parks, zoos, down the river or to see Father Christmas. These were the best days of my early childhood. I always got very excited about visiting them. I mastered the importance of friendship through them; my life would never have been the same in their absence. You become who you are through the company that you keep. Had I not grown up around them, I'm sure I would not have been as happy as I had been from that age. I feel they had left a true mark in my life. They say true friends come about once in a lifetime - I consider myself lucky because I've had mine there from the beginning.

I had trouble processing specific sensory information known as Sensory Integration Dysfunction. I was sensitive to sound, touch, light, taste, and smell. Too much noise or light in the playgroup room would make me squint and make me lose concentration in what I was doing. I hated people brushing past me but liked physical touch. The taste could too have been put down as very fussy eating but I do remember despising some smells. A couple of times, I threw up at lunchtime because somebody had been eating something in their sandwiches, which to me, smelt unholy. My mother then had to come down and pick me up.

Just beyond three years into my life, my brother, Rowan, was born. I remember sitting with my grandmother at the park while my mother was pregnant, and she asked me whether I wanted the baby to be a boy or a girl.

"I want it to be another beautiful little girl." she said.

"I hope it's a boy." I said feeling quite certain of myself. The birth of Rowan may have improved my confidence with somewhat significance. I felt older and looked up on as a role model for more competent behaviour. Rowan had long, curly, blond locks, and green eyes. He was also brought up under the same circumstances as I had, so surprisingly enough, he developed Selective Mutism too. I imagine that Rowan had picked up on my speech patterns and mutism so this was perhaps another factor which had influenced the Selective Mutism. As things went, it seemed fairly common for Selective

Mutism to occur amongst siblings. Rowan and I at any rate got along considerably well. We particularly loved to watch cartoons and play with toys together. At home, we were as normal as siblings could have been. I remember when he used to sit in the washing basket and laugh like there was no tomorrow. Around us, he was a very social little boy. It's a shame the same cannot be said whilst he was in public.

Unfortunately, things on the other hand did not seem to be looking too promising for us. All of our money carried on going down my father's throat in a form of alcohol before he came home blind drunk on most occasions after giving his liver another great kicking at the pub. That was exacerbated further by my mother bringing me up with my Selective Mutism symptoms at home such as my frequent temper tantrums, moodiness, bossiness, assertiveness, controlling behaviour, inflexibility, and extreme talkativeness on top of my other symptoms, whilst in public, I was mute. I hated being in public. I always had my head down around others.

"BLESS - look, she's gone all *shy.*" I would clench my fists every time somebody said that, and if it wasn't that, it was always, "*Jessica-*

this," and "*Jessica-that.*" I started to hate my name. The only people in my life who I was able to speak to addressed me by the name of *Jess* while everybody else I was unable to speak to seemed to address me by the name of *Jessica.* Strangely, since then, it had always been more difficult speaking to people who addressed me by *Jessica.* I had always wished people hadn't even acknowledged that I had been there which would have removed all anxiety from my shoulders.

Next, there were the troubles sleeping alone. I had always had a lot of nightmares and lucid dreams, and when I awoke in the middle of the night, I could not fall back to sleep alone again - a further noted symptom associated with Selective Mutism. I felt trapped even further by these nightmares. I would have nightmares of giant goblins chasing me, alone, down the alley, and trolls trying to get inside the flat. Silly, abstract dreams they were.

That goes without mentioning the irrational, generalised fears, even those of everyday household objects. I was afraid of a clock! It was just a simple wall hanging clock with an orange frame circling it, and when I would see it, I would cry hysterically and run into another room. It was the typography of the numbers which, I think, provoked the fear. This was also the case with ornaments about the living room. Irrational fears.

I longed to come out of my shell more than anything else I had ever longed for. I wished to wave my silence goodbye and embrace my fears. But unfortunately, I couldn't. The shell must break before the bird could fly.

Soon enough, we were moved into a temporary accommodation house. I loved that house. During the summer, Rowan and I would enjoy a picnic in the back garden with, laughably, a plate of potato alphabet shapes, waffles, and a bowl of bread. Why? It was because they remained the only foods which we would eat. We were extremely fussy eaters and had the most rigid eating patterns. I believe the anxiety was, again, the root cause of it. It caused avoidance in regards to trying different foods in the same way as it did with the avoidance of speaking. I was too afraid to taste new foods and my mother's patience with this must have worn rather thin before long because we were just too stubborn to taste anything other than two particular foods: certain forms of potato and bread. Ultimately, it affected our growth dramatically and we had always been the smallest in our classes all the way through school - smallest and quietest. That was a bad combination for a place like school. I, myself, was a bully magnet. I remember a time when we were at a restaurant and my father said to me,

"If you carry on eating so many chips you'll turn in to one. You start going yellow and skinny, and before you know it, you're a chip." I stared at him in horror. An image possessed me, of a rectangular yellow person, etched with facial features.

"I haven't seen those before." I said. He continued, "That's because nobody eats chips for *every* single meal, *every* single day!" Since that time, I faced the constant fear of turning into a chip each time I sat down for my next meal until my mother assured me with the news in the latter years that it was humanely impossible for a human being to turn into a chip.

It was a nice house in which we lived. The only house I had ever lived in. It had a swan tiled into the glass on the front door. Rowan and I had shared room as did my mother and my father. But as always, it came with its difficulties. Despite living there for half a year, we were not allowed to move a single piece of furniture, and there was mould growing in me and Rowan's room. In consequence, we pinned cartoon beach towels onto the walls to liven the place up just a little bit.

It was a norm for my mother, Rowan, and I to visit my grandmother every Sunday whilst my father went down to the local pool club. I thoroughly enjoyed these visits to my grandmother's. She had converted one of her spare rooms into a toy room for us which we took to full advantage. My grandmother spent hour after hour with us playing game after game. Sometimes, we would empty the shelves of every Teddy bear, form them into a circle around the room and played schools. I would always be the teacher so I could take the class register and teach the Teddies that were doing the things I'd dwelled most on wishing I could do - speaking particularly. The Teddies enjoyed it very much as far as I was concerned. At such age, I had an extremely active imagination. When I was alone with my imagination, I would quite literally be lost in my own new worlds. I travelled from the most inviting of worlds involving animals who found themselves lost in the wilderness under the living room table, Barbies surviving in the rolling waves of ocean blue during bath times, and my favourite Toy Story characters awaiting their fates at the hospital in the Barbie doll house. After our usual lunch of chips and the much ardently anticipated trip to the local sweet shop, we would then sail into other worlds of make-believe-play; perhaps *'Mummies and Daddies'* or *'Going to the shops.'* Since selectively mutes tend to show creativity tendencies, I myself, think this may have compensated for the limits of the most basic form of human expression – speaking. Therefore, this is, it seems, why sufferers tend to be so creative when it comes to expressing oneself. At this age, my future ambition was to become a hair-dresser, an ice-cream lady, or a vet. I used to give my ugliest, least favourite Barbie dolls a haircut and throw the hair out of the window so my mother would not find out. I used to draw on their faces too. I also took joy in being a vet, putting Teddy Bears onto my desk and treating them. As my own evidence has also suggested, it would appear that Selective Mutism sufferers show a huge love for animals. Animals, unlike humans, always seem to show love regardless of the circumstances. Had you had the hump with somebody, that person would usually ignore you for a short space of time, whereas animals, love unconditionally. Rowan and I both shared the love for animas. The amount of times I had begged my mother for a cat or a dog ...

To make matters worse, I went through phases where I stuttered with every sentence I spoke. The hardest thing for me was initiating my sentences as it was with the Selective Mutism. Often, I would drag the first syllable of the first word for about five seconds before the word eventually came out at the worst of times. As always, my brother picked up my habit of stuttering too. My mother believed I stuttered because I used to torment our cat. Expressive language disorders as such were also known amongst Selective Mutism sufferers. I believe it may perhaps have been the added stress of the Selective Mutism that had made me feel even more anxious and insecure when speaking which had brought it on. The stuttering seemed to go on in phases, but pretty soon from here, it dispersed.

Chapter Two –The Early Years –

My first day of school was disastrous. It had without doubt been the worst day of my life yet. I felt like an alien who had just landed on planet earth. I had not by any means considered beforehand how I would behave at school, in this instance, whether or not I would be capable of speaking. I remember the time when one of my teachers for that year of school came to visit me at home as a general school procedure. She asked,

"Are you looking forward to starting school, Jessica?" My teacher looked at me. I looked at her. I looked at my mother. She looked at me. I looked at the door.

"Talk then, Jess." My mother began.

"I wouldn't worry about it. She'll soon grow out of it; it's just a phase." said my teacher. This was the statement which had been said time and time again throughout the initial years of school. It was more than just a phase though, it was Selective Mutism ...

I went to Chesterfield school which was about a half hour walk from home. I believe you could say it was a good school at the time. It had an interesting history at the least ... The school had been built back in the year of 1897 and a considerable part of the original Infants building had been burnt down in an air raid during the Second World War in 1944. Although the children were safely sheltered along the edge of the playground, a teacher had lost her life because she had stayed behind to look for a child who had ran home in fear. The school building was very big and very historical looking. At the time when I attended, it was considered to be a reasonably good school.

I started school on the seventeenth of September, 1996, and to begin with, I attended every morning from nine O'clock until eleven thirty. Being left alone without my mother with a large group of strangers panicked and terrified me. I usually cried when she dropped me off in the playground every morning. I was constantly placed in an oppressive situation in which I could not make eye contact with anybody nor did I ever manage a smile. Eye contact was extremely threatening to me. My class mates always asked me the same questions every day, "Can you speak?", "Have you got a tongue?", and "What's wrong with you?" Can you imagine what that was like *every* day? To begin with, I was always alone during the course of break time. Our playground was equipped with sand pits, black boards, play time games, and we could go into a class and paint, draw or play. I never participated in any of these activities. Instead, I sat on the bench throughout the whole of break time. I had no friends, and even at the tender age of four, I was bullied. Two boys from the other classes in my year didn't really know each other but just took the bullying in turns. As I would be sitting on the bench alone, the smaller boy of the two would sit beside me and stare at me like there was no tomorrow. I would go elsewhere and spent a lot of my time hiding from him but he would always find me, follow me, and stand blocking my path. He never said anything, and it was beyond the question for me to. I even cried during these episodes but nobody ever see me. I was just a ghost, a ghost lingering around in the playground. The other boy was the same, only he was lanky and had a long face. He never stared into my eyes like the other boy did but followed me around all the same. He, however, used to strangle me in a playful manner away from the others. No matter how frightened and uptight I got, the words were still trapped tightly in my throat. I often wondered why they did this. But of course, I was a very easy target; I couldn't react to anything and was physically very small, in other words - totally vulnerable. All I could do was let the bullies have their ways when all of the while I would stand there miserably watching all of the normal children playing games in the playground with their friends. I felt so weak, vulnerable, helpless and different from every other child around me. I knew very well that I was completely different from everybody else, but I could not figure out why or how I could change it. It was just how I was.

After Christmas, I began to attend school full time. My teachers for that year were Mrs Sydney and Mrs Eva. They were very friendly and approachable people. Mrs Sydney had a mousey face, short ginger hair, and she wasn't recognised without her glasses. Mrs Eva, however, was noticeably older, had short grey hair, big round glasses, and often wore big, sparkly brooches. We were in Class One, and I distinctly remember how we had all different animals on our pegs with our names to hang up our bags and jackets. I had an owl on my peg. They seemed to accept the fact that I *'wouldn't'* speak and labelled me as being *'extremely shy.'* Things carried on pretty much the same for me. Yet, why were preliminary questions not asked after I had been mute after so many months? The human drive to communicate is extremely powerful and a few months seemed an awfully long time to be mute for. They said I would grow out of it. How wrong were they! Why would they not open their eyes? They were dealing with a four year old who never smiled, never spoke, and who rarely engaged in eye contact. The persistence, intensity, and avoidance were clearly much too severe for it to be perceived as simple shyness. It seemed ridiculous that nothing was done. They usually paid a limited amount of attention to me. The quiet child always seemed to have been the forgotten child since the teachers had always given their attention to the disruptive, naughty children. As the year progressed, I realised I was different from everybody else in my class in several ways: I had a very poor intellectual, social, and emotional development. Every morning and afternoon when the register was called, the teacher always had to look up to determine whether or not I was present,

"Jessica, it is very important that you answer your name when I call the register. You're so *silly*." Bloody teachers! If only they knew how difficult it was for me. My tongue was burning for the words to come out. And then, the whole class drank a carton of milk every morning during circle time, but me, since I hated milk. I was also very diffident when it came to crossing my legs when I sat down on the carpet. I remember looking at the ways the others sat thinking, *how on earth do they sit like that?* Every circle time on the carpet, I would sit there on my knees whilst the rest of the class would sit with their legs crossed. I also remember being unable to grasp a pen or pencil properly. I would clench my first round the pen or pencil when drawing or writing, and when I was shown how to do so properly, I didn't even consider trying because I convinced myself I could not do it. I also demonstrated difficulty when it came to making choices. Decisions such as 'Pick a partner', 'Choose a seat' or 'Think of a letter' proved me to be most indecisive. I was unsure about the 'correct' answer and didn't want to appear different to anybody else around me. This was also the case with non-verbal questions. I gather I was more or less afraid of my voice, not of what I might potentially have said. This may explain why bilingual children are quite susceptible to this disorder. The sound of my own voice repulsed me and I seemed to think it sounded very differently from the other children round me. I displayed difficulty following a series of directions and completing tasks. I can remember when we were asked to write out the directions of our journey from home to school. The teacher had come along to check mine when I had finished, and mine went something like, *Go out door, walk left, right, up, left.* In my mind, I could not process my journey to school, and because the teacher made me write more, I added some rubbish like, *I feed my cat, turn left, I get my toys.* The teacher then came along sometime later and I stubbornly covered my work up, closed my book, then hid it underneath another book and buried my arms on top of it. I knew my work was wrong. I *hated* getting things wrong, and no matter how hard I tried, I could never complete tasks correctly. As a result of all of this, I felt quite an aberration and disadvantaged from everybody else in the class. Yet, the teachers did take the responsibility to ask some girls to take me down to the toilet every few hours in spite of me not really needing to go there half of the time. At other times, not even the direst bathroom emergencies incited me to speak. I could not speak no matter how hard I tried any more than a person could be persuaded to not feel pain in an injury.

On the other hand, matters began to improve for the better when Nicole (who I had met at Toddler Group) started speaking to me and, thankfully, she turned out to be the select person whom I was able to speak to. She was a real life saver given my circumstances. Once, Mrs Sydney had asked me to read a short book so she knew where I stood academically with my reading ability, and seeing as I was incapable of doing so, Nicole was called over. Laughably, I ended up whispering every word of the book into Nicole's ear and she repeated the words back to our teacher. I can recall the laughter of classmates in the background at the time. Nicole was with me nearly every moment of the day. I would only speak to her when we were alone when nobody else was in the vicinity. The best way I can explain it, is that it feels as though it's literally illegal to speak; as if I was only programmed to speak only in the presence of Nicole. It does perhaps sound like stubbornness, and as much as it was, my throat completely closed up and the words were blocked up in my throat something like rush hour traffic.

However, Nicole could not always be there. In her absence, I was bullied by a brother and sister from the year above me. I was physically the smallest person in the school and they towered over me like giants. The girl had thick, chunky eye brows and bore a striking resemblance of a witch; she even had the nose. The boy had a slightly disproportioned face like a Frankenstein and they both made a habit of following me everywhere I went. They cornered me and stood around me fiddling with my hair.

"Do you want to play with me?" the girl would ask sounding a lot like the doll, Chucky, from the horror movie. Their intentions were simply to scare me, and they sure succeeded. They often made me cry and, owing to my mutism, whatever happened to me, stayed with me. I feel these on-going bullying incidents most probably influenced my bad dreams. I felt as though it was I who was in the wrong at all times and that it was my fault. It was my fault I couldn't speak, nobody else's. The guilt made everything worse.

We were always accustomed to many beautiful sunny days during the early springs of my life. Spring always showed her colours early whilst the liquid sun was constantly playing hide and seek amidst the clouds. These were during the days of Kathy. Kathy was a teacher assistant and dinner lady at the school and she was often on duty in our playground. She was very tall with very short, black, shiny, hair with tints of purple, and she wore a bit too much jewellery in my opinion. I can vividly remember the times when Nicole and I would hide and she was always the person who would come and find us and then chase us until she had caught us. Nicole found it hilarious. I hated it. She never gave me a break. Each play time, I wanted to be by myself or speak to Nicole alone, but instead, I had to put up with a dinner lady chasing me around the school. I can recollect this one time when I wanted to evade her because I had got sick of it so I ran to the girl's toilet and hid in the last cubicle slamming the door behind me. The steady rhythmic dripping of a tap and the rattling of pipes carried around the bleak and characterless room around me whilst I listened to the thudding of my heart beat in my ears. *She will never find me in here,* I remembered thinking; but I had thought too soon, there she was ...

"HMMM, I wonder where Jessica is,"

 "JEEEEEEESSICAAAAAAAAAAAA," she sang.

"Ooooops -" she muttered,

"– sorry -" " - where's Jessica?" She had peeped over the top of every cubicle, seeing as they were very low, before she had found me. I wasn't even safe in a cubicle in the toilet. I had been hiding in there for about five minutes and she must have seen me going in in the knowledge that I would not come out in a hurry. She was probably told to watch over me but what a great job she was doing! I remember a time after school one night when I was sure I had heard her outside my window. I immediately ran towards my wardrobe and hid inside it after convincing myself she had been out there until enough time had passed for me to be content with the fact that it hadn't been her in the first place. Paranoia had always been something which had seemed to affect me too, further influenced by the mutism.

To my mother's frustration, I refused to have my very first school photograph taken. I felt exceedingly nervous as I queued up with the rest of my class and further intimidated by the photographers themselves and the large photography equipment. I liked routine and change was one thing which panicked me. I queued up, and when I was about five people from the front, I pulled out and put on my stubborn face. I felt like a rabbit in a fox hole. I was scared. The most irrational of situations made me feel most apprehensive. It was just as well, either way, since it was nothing unusual for my mother to give me dodgy haircuts, especially cutting my fringe inches too short!

My teachers often took the approach of forcing me into speech instead of using techniques in order to decrease the anxiety. This only heightened my anxiety and negatively reinforced mute behaviour. They seemed to assume that I was slow to learn and that I was a bit dim witted because I did not communicate my answer to a question unless I was one hundred per cent certain that I was correct. This is because that was the fastest way to make the teacher to leave me by myself and get on with something else. I feel my cognitive and academic skills were hugely misinterpreted for this reason. What the teacher should have been doing was working on ways to decrease my anxiety because the anxiety was the root of the condition. Forcing speech from me just entrenched the condition.

I was making very slow progress with my fussiness with food and poor eating habits. My everyday Winnie the Pooh lunchbox always contained two sausage rolls with no sausage inside, a breakfast bar, and ready salted crisps. Every time I eat sausage rolls today, I am struck with nostalgia, recollecting the simple days as a young child. I could never finish the whole outside of the sausage roll anyway so I screwed the remainder of it up and stuffed it back inside the tin foil into a little ball. My auntie who had been a dinner lady at the school at the time took me down to the head teacher and asked her to give me a sticker for always finishing my lunch every day. I chose a bright red smiley face sticker to go on my yellow and white school summer dress. I couldn't hide my smug smile. I remember ordering a plain beef burger and chips at a restaurant with the family one weekend and I took the beef burger out and ate the bread roll and the chips. All I could do for weeks was boast that I had eaten a burger.

I was immoderately uncomfortable at school. I hated attention and I hated people. Nothing was ever done about my mutism. The only times I believe anything was ever brought up about it were at parents evening meetings where my teachers discussed my academic progress with my mother. My Selective Mutism was latent to her. She expressed her concern although she did not officially recognise my mutism as a problem since I had spoken so freely at home and around select people in select environments outside home. She often got annoyed with me about it. She used to say to me, "If you don't speak to your teachers, Jess, you'll have to go to a special school with a strict man teacher and kids with problems, even over the weekends, so you won't see me or Daddy." And always, "Do you know how ignorant you are! When people talk to ya,' you answer 'em, not stand there and gawp at 'em! Whassa' matter with ya'!" It is difficult to interpret the level of frustration I had within me. I was going through hell primarily being unable to speak. I was being bullied and often alone, on top of the problems at home along with everybody telling me I must speak. I was aware as to how important it was for me to speak. It was just speaking, how difficult could it be? But it seemed an impossible task. All you had to do was open your mouth and speak, and if you found it difficult you just had to push yourself harder and speak anyway. But it was nothing like that. It was like being trapped inside a brain which refused to co-operate. My throat went tight and while I was in the centre of attention in class it felt like the world had stood still just to look at me. In like manner, my stubbornness was simply beyond my control. The words were trapped in my throat like a mouse trapped in a mouse trap. When placed in an anxiety provoking situation surrounded by more than a few people, I would shut down completely and I didn't want to do *anything!* Anger radiated through me at these moments like a light bulb whilst I remained trapped inside this tiny cage of mine. I longed more than anything to shout until my throat run dry. Anger could not cover all that I felt. Even being undeterred by somebody whom I did speak to being present, I would suddenly switch to stubborn mode and go blank. Careless as I was of everybody around me, I would quite simply shut down. I didn't smile nor look at anybody and even at the expense of losing something or more importantly, somebody, from ignoring them with such intensity I wouldn't care any the less. Nothing in the world mattered to me at these moments and I was impervious to reason and another's presence. It was at times like these when Selective Mutism proved its most disabling effects. Nonetheless, I do not believe it ever occurred to my mother to take me to a doctor since she was told I would, in time, grow out of it, as many other selectively mute children had certainly been told. It made me angry. Since they all were adults they assumed they knew what they were talking about and that it was allegedly just shyness like other children experience when they begin school. But children eventually feel comfortable and settle in and would give you even a smile, but I did not. My anxiety was extremely specific to situations where I was expected to speak; I never stopped speaking at home and I was extremely stubborn. I think these were the three main factors which differentiated me from being extremely shy. I don't believe my behaviour was acknowledged by teachers as thoroughly as it should have been. I was never particularly seen as a red flag because it was not recognised as a problem.

In ways, I feel my mind worked in a way as it would have done as an autistic child. When shutting yourself down from all social interaction, all of your attention goes elsewhere. To the colour of the ring the teacher is wearing on her finger, to the Armitage Shanks logo on the toilet paper holder, and I would memorise every single word on the posters around the classroom. When very anxious, it helped if I did something with a rhythm to it. Like 'Left, right, left, right, left, right' or 'It's OK, it's OK, it's OK, it's OK.' I also displayed a condition known as Synaesthesia. I had a gender for each letter of the alphabet, numbers and colours, and I had a logo or a symbol appear in my head each time a day of the week popped into my head. For Monday, it was a logo on the front of a cigarette packet which my father smoked, a little train drawn on a piece of paper for Tuesday, a small wall for Wednesday, the Warner Brothers logo for Thursday, a Postman Pat ride down Waltham Cross for Friday, a big wall for Saturday, and for Sunday, a sun in the top right side of the picture. I also had a little picture or logo in my head for people's names. It was pretty much living on patterns. This, being another similarity between Autism and Selective Mutism, is how they can both be considered very similar conditions despite the main differences. When shutting down the social part of your brain, you begin to pay attention to the minor things which one usually wouldn't pay any attention to.

To say I had felt like quite an aberration would be quite the understatement. Although I was, I had always felt as though I was very different from the rest of the class. I don't believe I was ever given enough one to one attention with the teachers or set up with some of the other students in order to elaborate some of my social skills. I was quite a disparity compared to the rest of the class. As said previously, the silent child is always the forgotten child. The teachers just tended to leave me alone to get on with it as though I was going to grow out of it. I cannot stress enough the severity that nothing was done. After a while, classmates began to get the impression that I *wouldn't* speak and they therefore didn't expect me to. They always said "Jessica *can't* speak," and "Jessica *won't* speak." and I then began to associate myself as a mute which only reinforced the mutism. Correspondingly, this was very counterproductive because it made me less inclined to believe I *could* speak and the mutism became more entrenched meanwhile. It was majorly the expectations from others which rendered the mutism the most. This expectation caused pressure which of course made me feel more anxious, whereas with the absence of this, I felt more at ease. You are what you believe you are, and so when everybody around you has no expectation for you to speak, you begin to believe that you can't do so.

A year progressed, and as I began year one of school, Rowan began Play Group. He was indifferent from me. He had a couple of close friends more than I whom he spoke to selectively and he did not generally seem as withdrawn as I had done. When somebody would be asking him a question or speaking to him, he would, in most instances, look at them blankly whereas I would always turn in the opposite direction or look down at the floor. Rowan's eating habits didn't get much better either. He ate pretty much the same as I did - plain food. I do distinctly remember our love for Gingerbread Men. My mother would buy them every week.

I believe patterns of the mutism and whom children can and cannot speak to vary from child to child. Because girls, even from a young age, are generally more social than boys and girls tend to be more social, you would have thought that girls would be better off than boys would have been. According to studies, Selective Mutism is more common in girls than it is in boys.

The two problems my mother kept onto me about were my terrible nail biting habit and my skin picking. I imagine they were just maladaptive coping mechanisms to combat the anxiety which was so strongly possessing me. This invited many trips to the doctors. The worst treatment for the nails was a substance which made me vomit each time I went to have another anxious nibble. I used to swallow the nails too which resulted in threadworm which was by no means desirable. The skin picking, scientifically known as trichotillomania, affected me more than the nail biting. I barely even had any skin at all left round my nails.

One afternoon a week, we had a music teacher visit us called Mrs Francis. Mrs Francis must have been in her fifties. She had wiry ginger hair, fair skin creased with wrinkles, and thick-lensed glasses. She was known to the year group as 'The Lady with the Raisins' because she used to carry a flowery, tin pot of raisins around with her and when we were well behaved, we were rewarded with a handful of them. The class were very fond of them. When she came in, the class normally sat in a circle and played games, musical instruments, and sang songs. To me, it was all boring and insipid because I would never join in. One afternoon, the class was getting ready to play a game called *I went to the shop*. It was a memory game in which each individual had a turn to say what they bought and to remember what every other classmate bought. I never took part in any of these circle time activities and most certainly did not want to play *I went to the shop*. However, what was yet to happen left the class and Mrs Francis thunderstruck. Just before we started playing the game, for the first time ever, Mrs Francis pulled me aside and in a threatening tone said, "Hear, if you don't speak when you're permitted to do so, you will go outside and face the wall for the rest of the lesson and you will be in a lot of trouble! Do you understand?" Her words echoed in my head and then tears began to prickle the corners of my eyes. I began to cry. I had never been spoken to like that in my life. I had always been a reticent, little 'Goody-Goody' at school and I had never before been so scared. That was a huge threat to me. Only the *bad* children faced the wall outside and if I was going to be in trouble, would that mean I would be taken to the head teacher? The anxieties of this, for me, were incredible. I remember sitting in the circle crying silently, overwhelmed with a sense of indignation whilst the rest of the class took their turns. I was terrified. Not necessarily of the others reactions but just merely of speaking for the first time in my life around more than just a few people at once. How could I let people hear my repulsive voice? After dwelling overlong on my turn to speak, the moment arrived. I swallowed. I felt as if I had just swallowed a brick, my heart was in my throat. I remember feeling so angry. Then, it was as if my brain was functioning beyond my control. I spoke, "I … went … to … the … shop … and … bought …… a cat." The silence from the class was impeccable. Words fell like toothpicks as I spoke. The whole class stared wide eyed and gobsmacked. I had never before seen anybody grin as much as Mrs Francis did at that very moment. As I spoke, her smile broadened and broadened until she was nearly exposing her whole set of pearl white teeth, nodding her head fervently before she said, "WEEEELL DOOOOOONE! Everybody, give Jessica a big round of applause!" A rather lively burst of applause followed. I was in a state of confusion myself. I am yet to comprehend how I pulled those words out. I did not in fact really feel overjoyed about it. In fact, I didn't really care at all for I still felt horrible inside. From that moment onward, I could only initiate conversation, in other words, speak when spoken to and when asked a question, never spontaneously which meant starting a conversation myself. If nobody spoke to me all day, it meant I never spoke all day. When I did speak, it was in one high, shrill, hoarse tone, and I displayed no emotion in my voice and, spoke very laconically. I, like the vast majority of selectively mutes, could speak only when asked a question. Rowan had always been the same. It felt as if there was a strong force of anxiety pressed against my throat preventing me from initiating conversation. I suppose this is because when somebody is waiting for you to respond, there is expectation and there so no pressure.

In the meantime after school that day, Mrs Francis told my mother what I had achieved and my mother was very proud. My grandmother bought me a Spice Girls doll for it (from the former girl band) to go along with my voluminous collection of Barbie dolls.

Although everybody thought Mrs Francis had achieved a great deed in making me speak, it was actually perhaps for the worst. If I had carried on through school mute, it may have raised concern and I may have been referred to a speech therapist or otherwise another professional or specialist and diagnosed with Selective Mutism. However, people didn't know any better at the time and because I could speak only when asked a question, they had assumed I was just shy. I suppose it is the selectively mutes who responded minimally were particularly vulnerable to being overlooked given this reason.

I celebrated my fifth birthday relatively early due to our departure before we moved into another home so I could celebrate it with a bouncy castle in the back garden. All of my father's family were present, many from my mother's side of the family and friends of mine from in and out of school. In respect to the quantity of people there, I followed my mother around everywhere at the party and more attention was provoked onto me than I would like to have remembered. "Jessica ... bless, it's the *birthday girl*!" is all I was hearing from every direction. Somebody from my father's family stalked me with a video camera which did not by any means improve matters. There were times of the rarity when I did speak in front of others, but those were the times when I was comfortable amongst my friends; particularly on the bouncy castle and while we played pass the parcel. The best time was indeed the next morning after everybody had gone home. I was left to the left-overs of the party food and given the opportunity to view my presents. This, for me, was a huge social event. The only times I had been in social settings were at school and at the supermarket on a Saturday afternoon. Rowan and I were always very social at the supermarket. A lot of selectively mute children of a similar age had this is common as well. At school, because the sufferer was mute, there was no expectation from others for them to speak. Whereas, at the supermarket, nobody knew you, and so naturally expected you to speak, and so there was no pressure. In the event that somebody approached you in the supermarket and spoke to you then you would shut down like the drop of a penny.

We moved into our new flat after that. The flat was my idea of perfection, being very content there. It was on the doorstep of a park with wooden apparatus and, I, to my delight, occupied the most commodious bedroom with its own balcony on the second story of three. I was very happy with the park. It had many apparatus, and a grassy area just outside. The flat was just down the road from the last couple of homes. After a while, I met two sisters across the road from me, Fatma and Shana. We used to hang out in the park, on the street, at mine or their house, or took trips to the corner shop to buy sweets. We would buy penny sweets, jelly snakes, and ice poles. Every time we had a spare twenty pence, we would shoot off to the shop in our eagerness for sweets. A couple of days a week, their mother would cook some of the loveliest smelling foods and send Fatma and Shana to bring it round to us. And I remember, they brought over a few corn on the cobs one day, and for the first time in my entire life I said the words 'Thank you.' As mentioned before, I had always had great difficulty saying 'Thank you', 'Sorry', and 'Hello.' I am not sure what it was that rendered me to thank them, perhaps it was more than anything else for the reason that I opened the front door by myself, they then smiled and held the plate out towards me, and out of embarrassment of saying nothing and looking rude, I impulsively thanked them. I loved that park and the people who occupied it. They were the most fondest memories of my childhood.

Rowan started Chesterfield nursery as I started year two of school. He was also mute to begin with until he seemed to get to the stage when he, too, could only answer questions like I myself had. His teacher always kept an eye on him to make sure he wasn't being bullied, but as far as she was concerned, he, too was just a 'shy child.' With regards to the Selective Mutism, we were exceedingly alike by means of who we spoke to and our general behaviour. I do believe that Rowan's Selective Mutism was influenced and perhaps triggered by mine. He picked up on my behaviour and, as young children do, inhibit the same behaviours. This was quite common in other Selective Mutism sufferers in the same way. Round friends, like Tracy, Louise, and her now younger brother, Aaron, Rowan was as sociable as a normal child would have been. He spoke spontaneously, answered questions, and laughed as I did.

I started year two of school and had a new teacher called Mrs Wills. She was pleasant, although she didn't appear to be as approachable as my previous teachers had been. She had shoulder-length, shiny, blonde hair and a big smile. She shouted at me a few times, usually to speak up …
Every afternoon we caught up with our work that had been uncompleted during the day or during the course of the week, and this had all been kept in a particular, red tray. One afternoon, I was laden with four difficult pieces of unfinished work to finish so I buried the four books which comprised of the work at the bottom of the tray so nobody would notice since I was unable to ask for help. I spent the whole afternoon playing in my free time, and when Mrs Wills brusquely discovered my work hidden

at the bottom of the tray, she nearly screamed the building down at me. Of course, naturally, I collapsed into tears and even started shaking. I was an emotional wreck at that age and had always been emotionally unbalanced. I cried given any situation. I had always been very stubborn. I hated other people reprimanding me or telling me off even if I was in the wrong.

Academically, I was somewhat behind the rest of the class. I was exceptionally poor at English and mathematics. I had always *hated* mathematics with a passion. I just couldn't concentrate in these lessons since the different concepts and methods brought on so much perplexity. It seemed I had difficulty in understanding things. As difficult as it was to interpret, it was as if two different parts of my brain refused to work together. For instance, I would get half way through solving a difficult question in mathematics before my mind would go completely blank and I would have completely forgotten the method I had used to get half way in the first place. The mathematics suffered immensely for I couldn't ask for help and was rarely given it. I remember sitting next to the class mathematics genius one lesson and we were given a worksheet which was listed with difficult time's table equations. I copied his every answer, waited a minute or two to complete the final one which I had already remembered the answer to in my head, and approached the teacher just after he had done. It must have been shockingly obvious that I had copied his work, but in the next assembly, my classmate and I were rewarded with a certificate for impressive work.

I am grateful to say that I wasn't bullied anymore. The bullies moved on into the Junior's playground since they were now a year older than I. And that's when I met Shansel. One play time, I was playing at the sand table and a girl from my class approached me and asked me whether she could join me. Shansel was Turkish; she had shiny black hair which tumbled down her back girlishly and she was of course, quite a bit taller than I. She was very polite and we both shared similar personalities. Throughout the year, I became very confident speaking to Shansel and we soon became best friends. When Shansel and I were alone, I spoke to her as confidently as I did with my family. My confidence began to expand when she was there and when she wasn't, the ghost of my old self was back again. For the majority of the time, I was no longer living my life out in quiet desperation. We didn't want to hang around with anybody else; we had each other and made up our own games. I don't know what it was, but we just clicked immediately. I remember when we made up a game in which our aim was to get across to the other side of the playground without making any contact with the ground which we had made a habit of playing. I was so glad that we were friends and I no longer dreaded going to school.

My family and I went on several holidays when I was young and given that I had been rather young, I have a dim recollection of them, aside from one, which I'm sure I will never forget ... During our holiday in Tenerife, Spain, we spent a lot of time at our local resort area, Oasis Mango. It had an entertainment area where we watched things from Spanish dancers and singers to parrot shows, which was made up of a restaurant with two pools outside. Early in the day, we were settled round the pool area on the sun-lounges whilst I was in the kid's pool. I remember it distinctly. The pool had a large Micky Mouse painted on the bottom and the pool itself was surrounded by boulder-type rocks. I was rather bored in the pool since other than me, it was empty, so I decided to try something thrilling. Stupidly, and regretfully, I slid my armbands off of my arms, which kept me afloat, and put them around my ankles. Mistake. As I put the first one around my left ankle, I tilted to the left and with the aid of the edge of the pool I slid on the other. Not knowing any better, I expected to bob up and down with the armbands around my ankles half way into the water level. Instead, I was dragged down under the water by account that I weighed so little. I tried everything of my ability to pull myself back up above the water, but it just wasn't happening. I was totally vulnerable. My feet were thrashing violently above the water and I was very quickly becoming short of breath. Could nobody see me? I waited. Nothing. It's true what they say when your life flashes before your eyes. I was so sure I was about to die. I never stopped thrashing my legs, and in the meantime, I began to feel light headed. How could all of these people round the pool area not see me? At the time, I convinced myself that they could see me but they had assumed I was capable of pulling myself back up or just that they out rightly didn't care. There was no time for such things to cross my mind. I had such a deep desperation to suck up the longest breath of air imaginable. This was it. I had always imagined I would live for so much longer. As the last bit of air began to escape my lungs, something in my head just clicked and I began kicking at my ankles so hard that I didn't care whether or not they would break. I had never experienced such incredible anger like it in my life. BANG! I had managed to kick off one arm band with all of my strength and then did the same with the other. I lifted my head above the water and breathed in an incredibly long breath of air. I was completely dazed and dizzy by now. Breathing impatiently, I looked round. Impossible. My father was lying on his back on his sun-bed soaking up the sun; my mother was rubbing sun crème on her arms absent of her surroundings, while Rowan seemed to be (what looked like) fiddling with his fingers. I could not believe I was still alive! Tears formed in my eyes, doubling my vision. I was shaking, my hands furiously flapping like a flag in a strong wind. I was petrified and I felt sick. I limped over and sat on the sun-lounge beside my mother and pulled a towel over myself, still trembling like a leaf.

"What's the matter?" my mother asked most suspiciously.

"What's the matter, Jess?" my father repeated.

It was difficult for me to speak.
"I'm freezing." I breathed. As a matter of fact, I was indeed cold not to mention petrified.

Chapter Three –The Juniors School –

Given the circumstances, particularly the alcoholism, my parents split up at the time I had been seven years old. I had no complaints. I no longer had to sit awake at night trying to block out the sound of the fighting and the sound of my father shouting nonsense whilst he was drunk. Although, be that as it may, I did somewhat have my regrets about his departure. I must admit I thoroughly enjoyed those nights when we sat awake at late hours playing Rayman and Abe's Odd World on the PlayStation. To me, he was just a careless drunkard who put beer before his own family, and we were better off without him, but once he had gone, I lost my sense of security. I used to enjoy it when we both went shopping together on Saturdays and when he used to get us a Mcdonald's Happy Meal on the way home and allow me to swap my rubbish Happy Meal toy with Rowan's without him knowing. Naturally, I missed my father as you would. This nonetheless seemed not to help nor hinder my Selective Mutism situation.

With the aid of Shansel, my speech very much improved in year three. I began to raise my hand in response to questions during lessons. I was even awarded the title of most improved student of the term for 'improved confidence and participation in discussions.' Yet, I was still only able to raise my hand in answer to a question, and never to ask a question. I was only able to respond but not able to speak when it came to initiating conversation. My answers were also most minimal and spoken in quiet words. It sounds ridiculous, but that's the way it always was. I quite simply dealt with my anxiety by not speaking. Shansel and I often spoke to each other during carpet time at the end of each day while Mrs Davy read us Harry Potter and the Philosopher's Stone. I never listened to a word of this book and always sat clueless when Mrs Davy selected me to answer a question on it. Me and Shansel whispered random things to each other and were often in fits of laughter over nothing. We had a reputation within the class as being 'the two who only laugh.' We did live up to it very well. It was simply a mark of our friendship to laugh at and insult every little thing that was possible. Shockingly, I was even told to stop speaking and stand up for speaking during carpet time. A selectively mute told off for *speaking!* Unbelievable. Yet, should Shansel not have been there, my voice would have disappeared.

Shansel's old friends in the class had commented on how quiet and shy Shansel had become since she had been hanging around with me. It upset me deeply, because I knew, to an extent, it was true. We would always cup our hands round our mouths and whisper to one another so nobody else could see that we were speaking or hear our voices when we spoke to one another. It was a terrible habit and I felt I had been a bad influence on Shansel since she had been picking up on my speech patterns.

The following year also justified improvement. In year four, a new teacher by the name of Mr Grey taught us. He was a pleasantly amusing teacher and my favourite yet. He loved The Simpsons, and had the characters lined up along the window sill of the class room.

My English very much improved that year. My mother had always made me read and tested me on spellings each night. It was reasonable to admit my academic knowledge had strengthened in like manner. More significantly, my speech elevated with such intensity that I even began to speak amongst some of the other pupils within the classroom. Two boys sat at my table and we used to discuss the latest PlayStation games and how to pass levels on them during lessons. I found I was comfortable enough to speak to these two spontaneously although in defiance of the fact that it was very quietly. Opposed to the majority of selectively mute children, I had always generally found it easier to speak to boys than girls. I believe this was because boys generally seemed to pay less attention to you than girls did and it seemed they were less inclined to observe your reaction, removing the anxiety to speak. In other words, there was more expectation for me to speak spontaneously from boys. This may perhaps be why I became a Tomboy (a girl with male traits and hobbies).

Every Saturday morning, Rowan either went to his local football training sessions over the nearby field or played in a local football match. He never spoke during the game, nor did he ever call for the ball, and he only replied in small, quiet words as I did. He played in defence and never had the confidence to score a goal. This is the time in which my passion grew for football. Every Saturday, I would go aside on the field and have a kick about with the ball by myself. I used to look forward to these days throughout the week. I loved football immediately and I was very keen to teach myself. We always went with my mother's friend and her son, Sean, who Rowan and I equally spoke to very freely. After football, we would go on long walks down the river with them, playing football in-between and feeding the ducks, climbing apple trees, and visiting the horses. No amount of persuasion however from anybody else encouraged me to join a football team. My Selective Mutism told me otherwise.

I never had been a great admirer of my father since he was never able to maintain his promises such as taking Rowan and I out over the weekends and buying us presents for occasions such as birthdays and Christmases. As a result, in time, I became completely mute around my own father. By this time, I had only seen him on and off rarely over the years and I felt a bit intimidated by him after seeing him blind drunk only too often. His health was now deteriorating fast. My father would ask me questions about how I was and what I had been up to, and all I could manage in response was a timid smile. This behaviour was mutual between Rowan and I. I imagine it's because he copied me. My mother, my grandmother, and Rowan were the only family I was able to speak to. In the course of time, I never saw my father again.

Thereafter the many years of progressive speech, particularly in year five of school, year six was the year in which my confidence grew with the most magnitude. The Selective Mutism was undoubtedly still there, but it was sometimes absurd to think that it was still present. In class however, my speech was as poor as it had always been, but when it was just Shansel and I, it was different. We used to walk the corridors speaking loudly and laughing amongst ourselves when nobody else was around, and every play time, we would play Tag with a bunch of kids from the year below us. I used to be a very fast runner back in those days. I no longer hated school; in fact, I even looked forward to it because of Shansel.

Since I had always felt so confident and comfortable around Shansel, one day, I suggested that we could write a poem and read it aloud to the school in Friday's assembly. I whole-heartedly believed I could do it if I was with Shansel. Accordingly, we wrote a poem about a ghost who had a passion for toast after school hours. The following day we walked down to the head teacher's office with the poem and I asked if we could present it to the rest of the school in Friday's assembly; I could speak to teachers if I approached them and I wasn't intimidated by the head teacher. We were allowed. Students at my school never volunteered to go up in assemblies for the reason that they were only selected to do so by their teachers for appealing work. I do not know what was going on inside my head during the time, going up in front of the school like that … However, I was determined to go ahead with it. Friday's assembly was every Friday morning, but that day, it was in the afternoon. It was just as well because we had up until then to get excited about it, and when I started to speak to Shansel, speaking became easier. I remember it so well …

"Next, we have two girls from year six who have asked me if they can read their *fantastic* poem (- being a bit of an over-statement) to you all … if you can come up please, girls ..." said the head teacher.

Right, this is it. Please don't mess it up, I hoped to myself. But I knew I would not mess it up. Shansel was here, it was going to be OK. I drew a very deep breath of air, accompanied with the musty smell of the old mahogany flooring which shone with lustre, before I stood up. A wave of confidence streamed through my body. With Shansel by my side, I knew this was going to go favourably. I threaded my way up to the stage at the front of the hall with Shansel behind me in front of years: Three, four, five, six, and a hall abound of teachers. There must have been *over six hundred* people in that hall! As we stood on the stage, I contemplated the sight of hundreds of pairs of eyes all wondrously looking up at me at once. It didn't seem real, instead, trance-like. My heart twang like an elastic band readying to ping itself out of my chest into the sea of curious pupils who sat before me. It had beat very fast too many times before, but never like this. Everybody before me assumed I spoke and a fraction of them had seen me speaking to Shansel and had even got responses from me themselves. So essentially, they expected me to speak and I knew there was nothing to fear … and the words were there despite the semi-tightness of my throat. The silence from the school was absolute. It was like a vacuum, creating an overwhelming sense of emptiness within the assembly hall. I started to read. I thought I was reading incredibly loudly until the head teacher interrupted, "A little louder please, girls, we can hardly hear you at the back of the hall." I read considerably louder, but the people at the back of the hall could still hardly hear me. Despite my immense efforts, my throat felt too tight in addition for me to raise my voice any louder. I didn't care though; this was a huge achievement on my behalf. Shansel read the second verse, I read the third, and then she finished with the last. We looked up to signify that we had finished. The crowd burst into a rather languid applause.

"Very well done girls -" the head teacher spoke over the deteriorating applause, "- but *you* were a little *too* quiet." he said, gesturing me. *Too quiet?* A selectively mute had just read two verses in front of over six hundred people! It sure did not concern me about reading *too quietly.* I had been over the moon for what I had just done.

"I cannot believe we just did that!" I said to Shansel awe struck as we walked back down the hall. I *could* not believe it. I was buzzing. I had never experienced such a feeling in my life. We even had the cheek to approach the head teacher again in his office the following break time requesting a head teacher's award sticker. Shansel and I had always shared a childhood obsession with glittery, shiny stickers.

Sometime after that, there came a time when we got into big trouble. During a lesson, Shansel and I went down to the toilet. We often went down there to stand about and talk to waste a pointless amount of time of the lesson. This time, a girl from our class was in there called Sophie. Sophie taught us how to throw wet tissue all over the walls and the ceiling of the toilets. We seized hands-full of wet tissue before we pelted it in every direction around us. Poor care-takers. We were in stitches laughing and moderately hysterical. However, the fun soon stopped. It was perhaps the large transparent window of the entrance to the toilet which gave us away.

"WHAT ON *EARTH* DO YOU THINK YOU'RE DOING?!" We each stood rooted to the spot. Butterflies danced vigorously in my stomach. When we turned to look at how many wet tissues we had actually thrown, the laughing subsided. The room was smothered in it. The teacher eyed us accusingly then continued, "Here I am passing along the corridors, as busy as I am, to hear the screams of skiving pupils abusing the school property! Now who is your teacher?"

"Miss Davy." Sophie said tartly.

"*Preposterous*! I dare say I will be escorting you back upstairs to Miss Davy and informing her of your ill behaviour!" her eyes glowering malevolently. This was the first time I had ever been in any real trouble at school. The trip back to our classroom was a long one in which nobody spoke although I did seem to catch the teacher muttering under her breath such words like, "Such nonsense!" and "Ill-mannered children!" When our teacher was told, the three of us were made to face the wall in silence for the remainder of the lesson. Shansel and I did however not learn our lesson. Admittedly, at every chance we got, we hastily seized masses of tissue, drenched it underneath the taps before firing it all over the toilet like a cannon. We could not breathe from laughter. It made sense to us to do it again as if to compensate for the trouble we had been in.

Every year, each year group of the school participated in a sports day comprised of a long circuit of playground and sporting activities. Shansel and I volunteered to be the leaders of one of the groups of year three children and, miraculously, we were chosen. I just so happened to be the leader of Rowan's group. It was down to me to track the score on a clipboard and guide them to the following activities. I felt comfortable but I did not speak although there wasn't an awful lot to be said in any case. Our mother came to watch that day. To her horror, Rowan's group finished nowhere close to the top of the leader board.

"Why didn't you add on points? His team could have won easily." I quite frankly did not want to weaken my authority supporting favouritism. As common as it was found in selectively mutes, it seemed important to me to do what was right. Besides, chocolate and a certificate were nothing grand to boast over anyhow.

Everything seemed to be falling into place very nicely. I got into a local school called Lea Valley High renowned as a specialist sports college. Shansel was however going to another school which her sister attended. That was a great big disappointment for me because I knew I would not be confident at school without her. On the last day of Chesterfield school, Shansel and I got as many students as we could to sign our shirts and autograph our books and then we spent the remainder of the day enjoying the school party. I got some funny comments in my autograph book from some of the teachers. "Look, Jessica - please just be quiet!" and "Goodbye and good luck! Don't get into trouble next year for talking too much!" I saw the funny side of these comments. I had initiated the earliest school years surviving a year without speaking, to reading in front of the school in the eyes of over six hundred people. I was personally rather chuffed with myself. The factor which perhaps helped my speech with the most significance was Shansel. We just clicked. We both had the same sense of humour and stuck together every moment of the school day. In the case of the Selective Mutism, I think it had been advantageous that I had had one close friend other than a few friends to have stuck with. I must merit Shansel. She had helped me out a lot in terms of helping me to speak.

Chapter Four –The Seniors Downfall –

My first day of secondary school was a complete and utter downfall. I had been looking forward to it relentlessly all summer, but had certainly underestimated what it was really going to be like for me. I never fully contemplated my welfare at my new school nor did I think about whether or not I would find my voice, although I did feel hopeful about it. I packed my new school bag weeks before I was due to begin in anticipation and promised myself I would have a new, fresh start, make friends, and speak. I imagined a new best friend like Shansel would come along. Sadly, anything but ...

Lea Valley was a big, working class school with a prodigious building. The building was typical, old, and mundane, previously known as Bullsmoor School and was due to be rebuilt in the years yet to come. My mother walked me to school on that first day, and as soon as I had arrived, I grew extremely anxious and encountered so many mixed emotions that I just burst into tears that would not subside. I mopped my face then just let the tears have their way, and then when my mother had left, I felt like I was all alone in the world. She had taken my voice when she had left and I really did not want to be starting secondary school anymore. I did not have any friends, I was physically the smallest person in the school, and to top it all off, I was unable to speak. I simply could not force any sound out from my mouth at all. Words can hardly express how I felt. How I remember feeling so small, minute, surrounded by vast buildings and unfamiliar crowds of tall people. I was a little fish in a giant pond. All of the confidence which I had been most crucially gaining over the last few years of school had crashed back down upon me like a ton of bricks. It was like being in another world. I had had so many worst days during the course of my life but this was by far the worst yet. I just wanted to be swallowed up by the ground. Endless rivers of students walked right through me throughout the first day as if I were a ghost. I felt as though I just didn't belong there.

After being sorted into form classes in the hall and visiting our classes for the first time, break time arrived. As I had no place else to go, I sat in the canteen alone struggling to tear the web of silence. I waited for one of my classmates to recognise me and ask me if I wanted to hang around with them. Of course, they didn't.

Loneliness built a home inside me. Why was it I was the only person sitting alone? I thought my mother had reassured me beforehand, "Nobody is going to know anybody or have friends on the first day." That didn't appear to be the case. After the first of many wasted break times, the bell rang for lesson three. Panic lunged inside me. According to my time table I had history. History? Where on earth was that? I began to desperately walk the school in search of the humanities corridor. Every corridor looked the same, and in no time, I found myself lost. Two minutes turned into five, and then five minutes turned into ten. Luckily, a group of older girls eventually spotted me and asked me which lesson I had. Panic-stricken, I showed them my timetable which I drew out from my abnormally large suitcase of a bag and, thankfully, they took me to my history class. Bless them. I was so frustrated that I could not thank them. I had always had difficulty saying, "Please," "Thank you," "Sorry," and "Hello." and later, I was to discover that many Selective Mutism sufferers had this in common. Subsequently, I arrived at my history class for my history teacher to say, "Excuse me, young lady, why are you so late?" in a rather firm, stubborn tone. All I could do was look at him blankly. He frowned. *It's the first day for goodness sake. Can you not figure I got lost?* But before he continued,

"She doesn't speak English, sir." Somebody else said. That seemed to satisfy him.

"OK, sit down." he said, signalling a sit down sign, lowering his hand.

It was difficult to distinguish why everything fell apart that day. However, my anxiety had always been of the same intensity and the deprivation of the only aid that made me feel comfortable, Shansel, reinforced the Selective Mutism resulting in the most abominable consequences. I was in pieces by the end of that day. Expectations truly are a killer. I expected myself to have had a clean slate, to have spoken spontaneously, and to have made new friends, but when all backfires, you find yourself showered in nothing but utter disappointment.

The very next day, two girls from my class, Tina and Sharon, asked me if I wanted to hang around with them. I was in no position to turn down friends, so jumped at the chance to hang around with them. Tina was a down-to-earth kind of girl and it seemed we both had a lot in common. We generally had similar personalities and she, like I, loved football and was as stereotypes go, a tomboy. She had blonde hair, blue eyes and stood several inches taller than me. Sharon, was on the other hand, one of the friendliest girls I had seen in school yet. She was about the same height as I making us the two smallest students in the school. Sharon had long black hair, brown eyes and an unusually high voice. I was with them for the vast majority of the time, but at other times, they were unfortunately not always there …

Tina and Sharon had been with their friends from their primary schools one lunch time, and in the meantime whilst I had been looking for them, a group of intimidating girls approached me from a year or two above in the corridor.

"Little girl, where are your friends?" One girl asked me sarcastically. She had to be nearly triple my weight, perhaps even more. There were about five of them and they all circled me whilst I stood defensively against the wall. I was a bit confused and when they came out of the blue like they did I wondered what they were doing.

"How old are you? You look about *seven!* How comes you're such a *midget?*" They darted many stupid questions at me so I then pushed through them in an attempt to evade them and when I realised they were following me I snooped off into the girl's toilets just ahead. It was admittedly not the most ideal place to hide, the smell of disinfectant and cheap toilet paper hung in the air. Still, I desperately hoped they would not find me. I hid in a cubicle and locked the door behind me as I had done many times before by then, praying so hard that they would not find me. *Please do not find me in here. Please!* I begged. What I would have given for their pounding footsteps to die away ... I heard the voice of the big girl. My breath stuck in my throat.

"Where is this midget? Where are you, midget?" One girl asked.

"Open the door, little girl, we want to speak to you. Why did you push through us?" another asked. Butterflies invaded my stomach. They knew. They had obviously seen me go in there. I stood stone still behind the door of the cubicle. Before I had known it, one of them had climbed over the top of the cubicle on the right. Then, just as suddenly, another girl had done the same on the left. They poked their heads over, grinning sarcastically,

"Why are you *crying*?" they asked. I could not utter a word. When panic stricken, I would always shut down and my reactions and thoughts would be delayed.

"Tanya, she's crying." one of the girls spat. Tanya, the big girl, started laughing hysterically.

"What a baby!" For me, this was such a formidable situation. What was I to do? My heart was doing somersaults.

"Come out, now, before you make us beat you up!" Immediately, I unlocked the door and threw Tanya a dark look of sardonic hatred. If ever I had made a mistake, then that was certainly one of them.

"Did you just give me a frickin' dirty look you stupid little bitch?" Disgust wrinkled across her forehead. Before I could worry about Tanya, one of them behind me punched me hard in the back of the head. It really hurt and my eyes watered in pain. All of a sudden, incineration mounted up inside me and I just wanted to explode. Volcanoes were exploding behind my ears. Another girl pushed me hard against the wall. I eyed her contemptuously. The other girls gathered around her. Tanya spat in my face. My heart began to race much faster while the fire began to race more rapidly through my veins.

"Why're you creasing my mate for? You got a problem?" she asked. I was so helpless. I felt like a punch bag. I collapsed in tears barging through them and ran out thinking it be the most prudent thing to do. I was immensely upset and absolutely furious. I wiped the spit from my face and walked on hastily. I felt so stupid after that, they followed me round the school shouting abuse at me. I could not believe the abundance of students and teachers who walked straight past me whilst I was in tears. *Please notice me. Please.* But it was no good. I was a ghost to everybody else. Where on earth was I to go? Wherever I went, they followed. I had nobody; nobody would care if I was in tears. Since I had no place else to go, I stood outside the class of my next lesson, English, my face damp with salty tears. Tanya and her gang once more surrounded me.

"Where are your friends?" they would not stop asking me this same question. It played like a broken record in my head. I slumped heavily against the wall in exasperation, tears rolling down my cheeks. They closed up in a close circle around me, chortling at my efforts to escape their vicious circle. My eyes were darting headlights, scanning around my surroundings for any kind of sign for somebody to spot me. There were now about seven of them and they were each at least about two feet taller than I. I swallowed. The shock choked my throat. After moments of solitude, panic and abuse, people from my English class began to arrive nearing the beginning of my English lesson before the bullies walked away. After that, I just remember a crowd of people standing around me asking me why I was crying and what had happened. At this time, I was in shock and everybody was talking to me at once and I began to feel a bit dazed. I tried to distract myself, glancing at the posters pinned to the walls around me trying to distract myself with words; but it did not help. I started breathing impatiently, panting, my throat became even drier and I could not catch my breath. Only now I realise that was my first panic attack. It was disastrous. People just stood and stared at me like I was crazy. I felt as if I were being so stupid. *Grow up! Get a grip!* I told myself. One of my teachers told me to tell my mother, but that was unlikely to happen. A strong force of anxiety held me back, and if my mother found out what was happening to me, I imagined she would have been furious. Another girl from my class called Fiona told me I could hang around with her. Thankfully, she turned out to be one of the select people who I found I could speak to. She was a life saver. She took me to our head of year, Mrs Wilks, who told us to come back at break time the very next day so I could point out who the bullies were from the school photographs. That never happened though, because the next day, two girls from my class stole money from me during an English lesson so Fiona took me to our year leader regarding that incident. The bullies got away as always; nobody wanted to take me seriously. I realised you never knew how strong you were until it was the only option you had.

Fiona and I, in the meantime, become best of friends. She was a great friend to me. With the frustrations of people at school giving me dirty looks, bullying me, hating me because I was different, barging me in the corridors, and talking about me harshly in front of my face, Fiona even just speaking to me was a blessing. We did the most conventional things including sitting in the canteen, walking around or talking in a quiet place of the school. Tanya and her gang still bullied me on most days whenever they got the chance to. I tried to avoid them as much I could, but there were only so many places in the school one could hide. There was also another girl called Kayleigh. She was small, scrawny and had bleached blonde hair with a pointy mousey face. She was a close friend of Tanya's gang and walked home the same route as I did at the end of school. She seemed to get a buzz from screaming abusive comments at me most of the way down the road. Yet, as gaunt as she was, she still liked to push me around into walls and hit me before she ran away as if she was expecting me to run after her. Even beyond the school grounds, I could still not locate my voice when I had been by myself.

The teachers who had taught me that year typically viewed me as a shy girl. I was just the retard at the back of the class who never spoke. They never really acknowledged me in lessons nor did they pay any particular attention to me. Every parents evening meeting my mother and I were ever invited to, my target was always to be more confident or something along those lines.
"Jessica is very shy and her aim is to improve on her confidence." I got so sick of them saying it because it just was not going to happen. I didn't know if it was me being selfish or whether people genuinely did not even care about me. Why didn't somebody help me? I was perhaps the best behaved student in the class, and all I ever got was abuse from everybody else. As for one to one time from the teacher – forget it! Then there were the bad behaved students who prevented the class from learning and wasted the teacher's time. They were praised with school trips, sweets, certificates and the lot when they

were behaved. The behaviour I was displaying was just not normal. The Selective Mutism situation was just so confusing to me. Although I was content with the assumption that it was extreme shyness, subconsciously, I had known there was just more to it than that. I knew what shyness was. I knew how it felt to be shy. There had been times, in my other world, where I felt a little shy and the throat just didn't close up in the same way. It just wasn't the same. The words just would not escape from my throat. I literally could not control it.

The next year of school approached barely bringing about any change although Fiona untimely left the school. Two other girls called Lucinda and Judith started to hang around with Tina and I after this. This did not stop me from getting bullied though. A girl in my class thought it funny to trip me up, push me over to the ground and call me names. On the way to my next lesson coming out of the mathematics block one time, she pushed me over to the ground so hard that I cut open my arm while she and a group of her friends stood over me, laughing. I went to the toilet where I was alone, sick, and then dissolved into tears whist I tended to the gaping cut on my arm. I was so sick of these cold hearted idiots pushing me further down. A sense of unworthiness overwhelmed me. My confidence was sinking even lower. I felt like a sinking ship. As I remember, I was always feeling unhappy, worthless and like I never even deserved a place in life. Life ultimately seemed pointless to me at this point, it felt as if I had nothing ahead of me. I absolutely hated school. Putting my circumstances aside, it was a bad school at the time. A couple of our female teachers would burst into tears during lessons because they just couldn't handle the class when they were misbehaving. One lesson our Geography teacher walked out of the class and sat in the staff room for the rest of the lesson while the rest of the class continued to misbehave and chuck chairs at one another. Before registration in the mornings, my class would climb on top of the school buildings and smash the light bulbs on the ceilings of the corridors in the port cabins. People, on a daily basis, were getting jumped and mugged just outside the school gates and down the lane. At other times, students would set off the fire alarms when they had a lesson to their distaste so the rest of the school had to stand out in the rain for two hours whilst we were given a slap on the wrist as a whole school. Queuing up outside the canteen down the technology corridor was a living nightmare. We were packed in like sardines and there was the constant fear of getting crushed to death. In fact, one can barely even refer to it as a queue; just an enormous crowd of students ramming their way in once the double doors had opened. It certainly wasn't an ideal school for somebody like me to be attending.

Eventually, the school building was knocked down part by part before it was finally built into a new school building, and as a bonus, we were kindly given ten weeks off of school. The new school building was marvellous in comparison to the old one; the demolition of it destroyed the memories of what once was. It had been built in the shape of a stadium since being renowned as a sports college. The school was a colossal square with a courtyard which stood in the centre. Dame Kelly Holmes came to the school as soon as the new building was unveiled and the school's reputation was considerably better. The new building made me feel considerably more hopeful about school. Lea Valley High had always been an American school. The head teacher had also been American and we had to call our teachers 'Ma'am' and 'Sir.' The new corridors were bigger and brighter and I generally felt a bit better about school. The school, in general, were now generally better behaved.

Chapter Five – Further Anxiety Disorders –

In the meantime, the Selective Mutism began to bring on other anxiety disorders: I developed a case of Obsessive Compulsive Disorder (OCD). I went through phases of doing everything an even amount of times, usually two or four times or even up to twenty times during the worst of occasions when I was most vulnerable to anxiety. I pressed the light switches on and off twice, closed the doors twice, and all the same, other compulsive habits were checking whether my alarm was set at least five times before I went to sleep and checking that the hair straighteners had been switched off about a dozen times and then linger overlong on the fear that I hadn't switched them off all the way to school. I had to use the toilet about ten times just before I went out in case I got desperate when out and didn't have the opportunity to use it. There was no doubt that I was a perfectionist and I did not know how to stop until something was perfect, even if it meant trying tirelessly and overwhelming myself with frustration until something of concern was good enough. Domination was another symptom common in selectively mutes. My room, too, was spotless.

Everything had its own place, and if something was out of place, I would get stressed and angry until it was back in order.

Another deeper anxiety disorder I developed was agoraphobia. The phobias and fears in agoraphobia I struggled with involved activities such as leaving home, entering public places and travelling alone. In such situations, I would feel vulnerable and exposed to danger and what would happen if I was placed in a formidable situation I could not avoid? The worst part of it remained leaving home. Home was the place I felt most comfortable. I had my own space, my own privacy and I felt comfortable. Nobody was watching me there. Leaving home was daunting. I would be content as soon as I had readjusted to the outdoors after a while, but the simple prospect of departing was daunting. I dreaded the thought of the constant on-stage feeling I experienced and the desperate attempts to look normal in public. Being at home and being outside, for me, were like two different planets. That was the extent of it. More than anything, I did not want people to know I was afraid. It would stop me from going to places and doing things which I wanted to do. Saying no to going to parties and most social events was an impulse although I had always longed to go to them.

Social phobia was something which had affected me quite harshly. The only thing which mattered like the world was what people thought of me and what I looked like. My world practically revolved around these two things. Being teased, and particularly criticised, was like a punch in the face. I majorly disliked being introduced to new people, with the exception of being with my mates whom I never felt anxious with. I felt I was glued to the mirror and I would not be seen in public unless I looked my profound best. Time certainly made a fool of me. I wasted masses of it surveying my appearance and wondering how I looked in the eyes of others. My social phobia was of the same intensity as my Selective Mutism. I gather most selectively mutes develop social phobia or one or another anxiety disorders since their proneness to anxiety is so demanding and by reason that the symptoms of which are so starkly similar. In uncomfortable social situations, my mind literally could not process anything to say, no matter how hard I tried to think of more in-depth responses. Although I believe I did not have it to the greatest extent, it still made life extremely difficult. I would get uncoordinated and clumsy if I knew somebody was watching me and I would feel as if I was constantly on stage. I whole-heartedly knew people didn't really think nor care about me or what I was doing and I understood that I was just putting unrealistic pressure on myself, but despite this, no amount of explanation like this could convince me otherwise.

An acute form of avoidant personality disorder also stemmed from my extreme anxiety. Known to be a condition characterised by extreme shyness, feelings of inadequacy and sensitivity to rejection, I believe I suffered with it affecting me more severely at times than at others. Despite my knowledge that it was not so, I felt inferior when compared to others since my confidence had been dragged so low. I would automatically assume that new people whom I would meet would be thinking negatively of me and I would constantly be under the impression that I was not an approachable person. These thoughts would therefore lead me to shutting down completely. I suppose my facial expression may have played a part in this too. When you automatically fix your facial expression into a miserable one, people just do not want to know you. The moment people see you, they judge you by the way you look, and the moment they decide they don't like the way you look is the moment they don't get to know you. This was what made me so paranoid.

Naturally, it was like a propensity to develop other kinds of anxiety disorders since the anxiety affected me so intensely. It was perhaps just a matter of triggering it. I believe Selective Mutism and social phobia are very alike and I would imagine that nearly every individual suffering with Selective Mutism had social phobia. It is said that ninety per cent of Selective Mutism sufferers also suffer from social anxiety. I can further concede to having developed seasonal affective disorder (SAD) during the worst times of the winter, in particular. The lack of sunlight and the short winter days often brought on a minor form of depression and made me tired and moody at the worst of times. I therefore made it my priority to get an appropriate amount of fresh air each day and to be out in the sun as often as it were possible. As I grew older, it did subside to some extent although I was still unnecessarily tired through most of the given time. I would be living on cloud nine when the day dawned a brilliant blue, cloudless sky alongside the burning sun. It was strange how the one simple prospect of the weather had such an incredible impact upon my mood. It would make me feel extremely hopeful, optimistic, and happy about the day ahead. In opposition however, dark, cloudy, rainy days brought on my agoraphobia and welcomed my miserable, moody self.

At home with my mother and Rowan, I was bossy, stubborn, moody and assertive. I had dramatic mood swings, crying spells and exhibited a lot of procrastination. The amount of arguments this caused ... As far as I was concerned, I was always right and everybody else was always wrong. As for the procrastination, I didn't know how to live in the moment; everything was left until later on. Homework ended up getting done in the last five minutes before I left for school, my room remained messy for months at a time, and everything else which had to be done within a particular time frame got done in the very last moment. I felt I expressed an inner need for control because, elsewhere, I had none. At home, I don't feel I was a very pleasant person to live with.

Chapter Six –Selective Mutism Uncovered –

It had been I who had found out about Selective Mutism by complete coincidence. I had finally found a way to address my silence during year nine of school when I had been thirteen years old. One evening after school, I had been watching television and had been merely flicking absently through the channels until something snatched my attention, "- is unable to speak at school." I caught as I flicked forward to the next channel. Anxiety, like a cancer, grew. I flicked back anxiously. I sat there, in deep wonder, with my eyes glued to the television and the remote gripped uncomfortably firmly in my hand. I was just certain this was not about shyness. I knew this applied to me and would be of great fascination giving me some answers. I was feeling more apprehensive than ever before, intrigued to hear more. Nothing could have prepared me for what I was to hear though. The documentary proved to be about a young girl and her younger brother with Selective Mutism, just like my brother and I. It tracked their daily lives in and out of school. I sat there seeing myself through the screen, dumbstruck. My heart dropped like a stone. Questions and thoughts then exploded in my mind. This seemed quite serious. I had a disorder? No. Not me - no way. I could not register the fact that there was something actually *wrong* with me. Immediately I was certain nonetheless I fell under the category of selectively mutes. There was absolutely no doubt about it. Deep down, I had however always known that there had been a very good reason for my behaviour at school. Everybody always put it down to shyness, but it just felt like as if it was a lot deeper than that. It was not the same as being shy. My speaking patterns were extremely complex and there included certain rules regarding where, when, and to whom I spoke to. The difficulty speaking was directly related to the expectation to do so. The expectation then made me feel nothing but panic that sent a physical paralysis to the vocal chords. The persistence, intensity, and avoidance were much too emphasised for it to be dismissed as shyness. The other feeling I felt aside from dumbstruck was *absolute relief!* I was immensely relieved that it was not my fault I found it almost impossible to speak under select circumstances, particularly at school. I remembered the first day of every new term when I promised myself I would have a new start and speak. It was just speaking for goodness sake, how hard could it be? I would get home after school that same day and hate myself after kicking myself all the way down the road because I could not do it. Apparently, the disorder was found in six in every thousand children. And then it hit me like a ton of bricks. How could nobody else know? How could I be the only person with Selective Mutism and yet the only one who knew it? Was it fate for me to see that documentary? That was when I realised that Rowan had Selective Mutism too. The awareness of it must have been disastrously low. *'Children have a tendency or vulnerability to develop the disorder genetically.'* My mother, in my opinion, seemed to show signs of anxiety frequently and my father was solely responsible for the stressful anxiety risk factor. I knew almost immediately. It was sod's law that I had to find out this way. The position I was in ... What was I to do? I could not tell my mother, it seemed an impossible task and for a reason beyond my knowledge, I did not want her to know either. This seemed to be because I was initially very embarrassed by finding out I had a disorder and I was too afraid to receive any kind of treatment for it. I was simply too afraid of myself. I was ashamed too, because I was different. I didn't want absolutely anybody to know that there was something mentally wrong with me because they would laugh and not like me. At the time, this is how I saw it.

Immediately after, I researched Selective Mutism as much as it was possible and I was truly assiduous about it. It had become a passion in no time. Reading information, I was amazed at how correct and accurate it all was. It was like putting together the puzzle of my life. I had always wondered what had caused my severe separation anxiety, my difficulty sleeping alone, my introspectiveness, my many temper tantrums, my many fears and, most importantly, why I could only speak to select people in select social settings - those being just some of the symptoms. Amid the excitement and euphoria, I wanted to make it my mission to find more answers, help spread awareness (with the exception of the people in my life) and to support others. It actually fascinated me to say the least and gave my life some meaning.

After having found out about Selective Mutism, my life carried on indifferently to that of which it had done before. I believe the only things my awareness of it had changed had been the feelings of indignation and resentment. How could nobody be aware of my dark world of forlorn despair and fear? How? I was always upset, I never spoke, and I had no friends. Why did nobody want to help me? Why did none of my teachers find this the least bit curious? My voice was trapped so how was I supposed to tell anybody? At such thoughts, hot rage burned in my veins. I was a thunderstorm about to explode. It made me so angry. I didn't know how much more repressed anger I could hold within me. The simplest thing to have done was to have just told somebody, or failing that, written it down and shown somebody. It wasn't the simple fact of doing it, it was initially all because of the shame and embarrassment.

Chapter Seven – The Summer Uplift –

My younger cousin, Molly, (who was four years younger than I) lived down my road and persuaded me to come to the park outside my flat one day after school. I believe I stopped playing out when my friends across the road moved away, and like everything else, it soon became an inhibition to stay indoors again. Molly had short straight brown hair and hazel eyes. We got on rather well as cousins and I was able to speak to her confidently most of the time. Molly introduced me to some of the other kids down our road who were regulars at the park. To begin with, I was very quiet and withdrawn, but after a while, since I had first met them in small groups, I was able to speak to everybody spontaneously. I am pleasantly pleased to say that after spending so much time with the people from down my road, I grew very confident. I started to shout, laugh, and talk all of the time and I had never in my life felt happier. My confidence rose dramatically. It had been one of my highest points. Yet, I wish the same could have been said about school. The bullying continued and I spent my days locked in my endless world of solitude, silence, and fear at school and then at the end of the day to my other world of freedom where I was confident, content and happy. Every day, I was quite simply slipping in and out of my two worlds whilst everybody around me knew no different.

My summer was most splendid. I savoured every single moment of it. The moments of freedom. The birds in the sky. The sounds of the aeroplanes flying across the sky on a sunny day and the many debates about the very high up ones which left white smoke tracks behind so-called weather forecast planes. The sights of people walking their dogs, the laughs of children playing Frisbee in the park. The soft breeze. The sweet taste of lemon ice lollies and Coke in the sun. Life is made up of moments. Moments which mean it all. Amongst some of these moments, my mates and I played football every single night, along with run-outs, hide and seek, twenty one dares, we raced, had water fights and had late night conversations on the swings at the park. I remember the night we see a shooting star bolting across the night sky on a starry night.

I went out with my very first boyfriend at the age of twelve. The one relationship which I knew I would never have liked to forget. I remember the dance song *Fly on the Wings of Love*, I was the first one to get that song on my phone, and soon, we all had it after sending it to one another via Bluetooth and, to me particularly, it had become synonymous with the park and all of the people in it. It wasn't a particularly rigorous relationship, pretty childish I thought, but he still meant an awful lot to me. I remember when he would jog out of his flats across the road dribbling his football like a knight in shining armour and my heart would start racing and I could not disguise my smile for anything. He made my confidence soar. Most of my happiness stemmed from playing football and my friends. I was not used to being round loads of people whom I could talk and have a laugh with. Really, it was just a normal council estate flat situated in a normal, boring area. But when you spent your days locked in a different world of solitude, hurt, anger and no love, it was heaven to me. There was no place better in the world to me.

My mates and I went down to Spider Park every other day. Often, we used to split up into the same two teams, commonly of about six a side, and fought a war as we called it. On each side of the field, we made our own bases and decorated them each with anything we could find. Our base was in the forest area and it housed a table with three legs and another stick balanced underneath it along with a couple of chairs. Our table even had a table cloth on it. Then we charged at our opposing teams with sticks, poles and whatever we could find and fought our war. Our aim was to take over each other's bases in an attempt to steal their possessions. It was immensely entertaining. It rendered so much laughter.

I was fairly popular amongst my friends and definitely the most garrulous. I was very talkative and always spoke my mind. I had never been ashamed to say what I wasn't ashamed to think. I always had something to say and could not repress my silence for any longer than a minute. It was just no fun keeping quiet, there was just too much to be said at every one time.

One of the most memorable times of that summer was when we got Elbert to believe in spaceships. Elbert was a bit on the credulous side although I did express my sympathy for him. Nevertheless, he was a bit attention deficit and a pain in the backside at times. We used to pretend that there was a spaceship around the back of my flats. We would run away, hide from him for about ten minutes, and then return pretending that we had been to space and encountered aliens who wanted a word with him. The poor boy fell for it. I felt I was a reasonably good actress too, having the ability to make any situation seem totally believable due to my introspectiveness.

"Elbert! The aliens told us they want a word with you. Their spaceship is waiting around the back of the flats for you." He took in a sharp intake of breath.

"*Aliens?* What do they want with *me?* What do they *look* like?" he asked with an expression of utmost awe etched upon his face.

"Yes! We don't quite know, they said they wanted a word with you. They are tall, pink, jelly figures with huge tennis ball-like eyes. You need a password to enter." He stood absently scanning the sky for perhaps the sign of another space ship, his mouth hanging open, apparently lost in thought. I brought down a handful of mini Mars bars from a box of Celebrations and gave them to Elbert claiming another alien from the planet Mars had given me them and that there were hundreds upon hundreds of Mars bars up there. He had the word gullible written all over his face. It was, in the long run, entertaining to spark his imagination and open his mind up to unlikely possibilities of UFO's.

My world revolved around that park. It was one of the only places I was happy, being surrounded in a playground doing things you enjoyed in the company of people you could speak to confidently. Even on the summer days when it rained like a rainforest, we would roll around in the pool sized puddle dripping wet. In the evenings, my best friends Nick and Fred would be absorbed in conversation whilst listening to the Mortal Combat theme tune over and over again until it played in our heads like a broken record. My confidence just came so naturally in these sorts of environments. I would completely forget that I could not speak at all when absorbed in enjoying myself and chilling with friends.

Chapter Eight – Year Ten –

Of course, the summer holidays unfortunately didn't last forever unlike the memories I had encountered. I felt I had gained so much confidence over the past six weeks, but it all fell back on top of me once again on that first day back at school as September rolled on. Back to square one again. It was very difficult having lived such a normal life for six weeks in confidence and then going back to school with no indication from others that I was even existent.

The only other two people I spoke amongst spontaneously at school were Tina and Sharon, particularly Tina. Lucinda and Judith did often wonder why I spoke to Tina and not them and often made the assumption that I only liked Tina, but of course, this was not so. It seemed absurd to be able to speak to only one of the girls spontaneously, but that's just the way it always was with Selective Mutism: I was only able to speak to select people in select settings under select circumstances. They all believed me to be oppositional and stubborn and it was extremely awkward and frustrating to me at times. In my opinion, there fell about probable reasons for this. I am forced to believe it may have had something to do with the expectation from others which changed the ways in which each individual reacted to me, spoke to me and their general presence around me. I found that I could usually speak spontaneously around the few individuals who would always look ahead or in a different direction when waiting for me to reply verbally. I more or less felt as if they were not really judging me and they would henceforth be treating me in a way as if I had always spoken. This is why I believe it is so vital in treating the selectively mute as if they had always spoken because you're then expecting them to speak. An example of one of these individuals was Tina. Nonetheless, Lucinda and Judith generally looked at me in a more scrutinising manner, as a polite gesture, when I would be about to reply verbally to them and sometimes, they also displayed that Oh-my-God-she-is-speaking kind of look on their faces. So, essentially, the mutism changed from, as well as setting to setting, person to person.

At school, different subjects provoked different moods. I had always had a passion for English. My love for English conquered the likings of any other subject. My English teacher, Mr Michael, was the first to discover my talent at essay and creative writing. He had been my favourite teacher of all and he always acknowledged that I was in the room. Like every other teacher who had taught me, he seemed to think nothing very much of my mutism. I was just 'shy' to him. Whenever possible, he excused me from participating in group work since he knew how uncomfortable this had made me, assisted me with my work individually and he could automatically tell when I had completed the work which was almost always before the rest of the class. I was very disappointed to hear he wasn't going to be my teacher the following year. Leaving all of the social interaction out, everything went into the academics instead. I'm assuming this is where my love for English came from. Mathematics - need I say any more! I hated it and it seemed such a waste of my time. I just could not focus and was often confused by everything. Along with this, it was always in mathematics lessons that a dazed feeling would come over me. It was harrowingly unwelcome. When this came over me, it felt as if it wasn't really happening, as if it were a dream and simply unreal. It didn't occur frequently but at the times and when it did it was distressing. It would last for no more than thirty seconds and it caused moments of great apprehension. I was unable to even think properly. An addition to the problem had been the fact that I had always been in the bottom learning sets for the subject with all the disruptive pupils and this neither did help. Listening to the conversations of others and day dreaming had become a habit of mine during my mathematics lessons. The only other thing I did aside from this was observing everything that was going on around me.

Although Physical Education happened to be my favourite subject, at school, my Selective Mutism had made it my least favourite. This year, I just so happened to be undertaking a leadership course and the exam involved children from nearby primary schools coming to ours and we each had to teach our own class of children consisting of around thirty pupils. *Perfect.* My Physical Education teacher was very good and she could be very pleasant when she wanted to be. Despite this, I disliked her for other reasons. Understandably, she often had a go at me for not speaking, but when I actually did speak she carried on and I think she went a bit too far. She made me stand half way down the tennis court and made me repeatedly shout my name until she thought I was loud enough. With Selective Mutism and being in an uncomfortable situation, there's only a certain pitch your voice can climb to since the throat starts to feel too tight and I was shouting my name as loud as it got while sharp daggers of anxiety ran through me. I was extensively proud of myself, for one, I actually spoke and two, I shouted at a considerably loud pitch. But no, that was not good enough for the likes of my teacher. She stood on the opposite end of the court shouting,

"SHOUT! WE CAN'T HEAR YOU DOWN HERE!" The humiliation was terrible. The class were in stitches laughing at me and it seemed she found it funny too. If the leaves on the trees around were shaking a lot, it was nothing compared to how much I was. My heart was racing out of control and it wasn't pleasant. Another lesson she asked me a question regarding a rule of netball and since I did not happen to know the answer anyhow, I shrugged my shoulders.

"EXCUSE ME? DON'T SHRUG YOUR SHOULDERS AT ME! THAT'S SO *RUDE!*" I dreaded her lessons and having them three times a week did not improve matters. I didn't turn up for the exam, believe it or not, and she sure had a crack at me for that before she told me to go away because she didn't want me in her lesson any longer "So rude ..." she muttered as I left the AstroTurf. I had much to say about 'So rude.' I spent the remainder of that lesson having a silent cry.

I chose to study art that year to let my creative side shine through. I wanted to study Physical Education but there was too much communication involved. I enjoyed art, but I didn't necessarily enjoy the practical parts. I hated using the pottery machines in front of the others and I didn't enjoy painting either which compensated a huge percentage of the work. We as a class were shaping wood one lesson with a sharp art tool and my finger slipped resulting in a nasty gash in my thumb. The blood streamed out relentlessly and I couldn't for the life of me approach the teacher. I sucked the blood away but it still streamed out rapidly. Luckily, the girl beside me noticed this and informed my teacher allowing me to clear it up.

Because I was now in year ten, I was obliged to undertake a weeks work experience at a selected business. I chose to work at a local veterinary practice. I knew I would scarcely be able to speak, but aside from that, I genuinely did enjoy it. There was a lot of observation, and not a lot of work. I sadly had to watch an old, ill dog being put down while its owners stood beside him in tears. I held the tears back. It was the saddest thing I had ever witnessed in my life. A single injection, and within the blink of an eye, his life was gone. I helped wrap the dog up and then carried the body into the freezer. It was one of my least favourite experiences when working there. I watched animals get castrated and get operated on as well. I praised myself for having a strong stomach. Other duties included cleaning scalpels etc, bird cages, and work surfaces. As always, I responded minimally and only when asked a question. If I was unsure or curious about something, I could not ask a question.

I was still bullied on the seldom occasion at school despite having a group of friends round me on most occasions. Such a time occurred when a boy in my class slapped me in the face for not answering him when he asked me why I never spoke. I was absolutely furious. My cheeks stung with rage. He had almost always given me a hard time … Astounded as I was, he started a rumour which spread around the year that I didn't like black people just because I couldn't answer him. Did he think he was the *only* person whom I did not speak to? The rumour spread like the plague. Soon enough, people for a while were constantly asking me whether it was true. All I could do was shake my head to prove it wasn't. I was furious and overwhelmed with indignation. There were times when a younger student spat in my face down the design and technology corridor and a further time, another invidious younger student threw a plastic cup of water in my face because they didn't approve of the crowd I was sitting with one lunch time. This invited another panic attack, this time alone in the girl's toilet. I had never felt so violated.

Tina, a boy called Eddy and I were seated at a desk with a supply teacher one science lesson. Eddy was a most immature boy, not to mention arrogant and most egocentric.

"Sir, she said she saw you picking your nose." Eddy said to our supply teacher. The supply teacher turned to me with a look of questioning scrutiny crossing his face, awaiting a response from me. There was a long, uncomfortable silence between the four of us. My expression was blank, unreadable. They all looked at me - Eddy and Tina, smiling. I looked at Tina hoping she would defend me. She laughed in a friendly manner.

"Just ignore her." He said after a long moment. I felt awful. Unsurprisingly, he never did come to assist me with my work that lesson. What a fool I must have looked.

During registration class my friend, Lucinda, and I, used to go on to a friend's social networking website on the computers and speak to each other via a chat room despite being seated next to each other. She was one of my closest friends now at school and I hung around with her on a regular basis. Lucinda used to ask me how I was and what I was going to do after school and stuff of the similar sort. Apart from rarely by text, this was one of the only ways we ever did communicate.

Chapter Nine –Year Eleven –

Away from school, I had soon become an extrovert and I'd grown much more confident. Football and sports turned into my passion and this is how I expressed myself and let out all the anger that swelled up inside me like a massive balloon. I was soon to have discovered that I had considerably agreeable leadership skills particularly with younger children and they proved to be beneficial when I went out to play football. It came natural to me to motivate and encourage others.

A day never went by without me playing football - *ever*. I would rush home from school almost every day in the excitement of my yearning to play football. I wouldn't even walk along the pavement, I would go underneath the bar fence on the grass so I could get home two minutes sooner. My physical education told me I was an amazing footballer and that I should play for the school team. I hated the sound of that, yet it took a hell of a lot of persuasion before I actually did consider participating in a match. I didn't very much like girl's football since I had grown up from an early age playing it alongside boys, this was the first time I had ever played girls football before and girls played too violently. Playing rough was no problem, it was just not going to work in an uncomfortable setting in which I shut down. We played away down Harrow against a team called Great Heart girls. I had to admit, they seemed to play a lot better than we had. I didn't get many touches of the ball since I never said a word. I ran up and down on that field like a dog and found it a great struggle to play being in an uncomfortable environment with the feeling my Selective Mutism gave me when it felt like the world had stood still just to watch me. I was so disappointed by the end of the game. I didn't want to play in any more matches after that and the girls eventually stopped telling me when we had matches so it was just as well. My first thought after that game was, *I'm forever done with football.* I was a failure. I was proud of the fact though that I had brought myself up playing football without ever having been to a single training session and playing in just one match. I soon became tired of coming up with excuses from the countless people asking me why I didn't join a football team. It was always, "I'll probably sign up next season."

Alternatively at school at the age of fifteen I practically stopped speaking all together. I was sick and tired of everybody making assumptions as to why I didn't speak and not liking me owing to this reason. The boy in my form class who started the rumour that I was racist because I didn't speak to him soon made me go downhill a degree. It then became a lot harder to start speaking again. I had now become accustomed to being completely mute. I was really unhappy at school the vast majority of the time. Nobody wanted to help me so why should I speak to anybody? I cannot put enough emphasis on how frustrating it was. It was almost *incredible* that nobody knew what I was going through. Fire raced through me at such thoughts, widening my frustration in to resentment and anger. I was so angry and upset that I used to shake from it and I almost started to convince myself that I didn't even *want* to speak. It struck me as such an outrage to the extent at which I was dismissed. Which fifteen year old *'shy'* girl was *conclusively mute* at school? I understood that the awareness was very low, but how could professionals such as teachers be *that* ignorant towards it? I think the problem was perhaps their misinterpretation of what the mutism was. Defiance and manipulation is how it probably looked in their eyes. My stubbornness, I think, was caused by everybody around me pressuring me into speech growing up. As reflected in many other cases, pressure is the very worst thing you can put on a Selective Mutism sufferer. You cannot punish or physically make a child do something which they are actually incapable of doing.

My teachers were this year once more no more oblivious to my problems than the previous ones had been. My history class was comprised of a particularly small group. There were no fewer than ten people in this class and there were rarely this many people in the class at once owing to frequent absences. As a consequence of very few people being present, it was more difficult for me to obscure myself and I was more often expected to speak. My teacher of history, Miss Tell, was a very much respected and smart woman and I was pleased when I took the first glance at my timetable on the first day back to see her name. Miss Tell's lessons were very educational and yet to my great dissatisfaction also very social and verbal. It was also in these classes I felt lonelier than I had in any other of my classes amid the class all sitting around one small table during a numerable amount of lessons. One lesson when we were writing our coursework, Miss Tell told me to stop writing and to inform her when I had finished a particular paragraph. I waited for no less than twenty minutes whilst being unnoticed because I had no way of indicating that I had finished before I proceeded on to the next paragraph myself. Ironically, it was almost a minute after I had started writing my next paragraph when she came along, "Why did you carry on writing when I specifically told you not to until you let me know you were finished?" she said half-shouting in a stern manner. I swallowed. There were tears in my eyes but I daren't let them escape. I hated it more than anything when people shouted at me when it was so hard for me to speak. It made me shake with anger. Away from school, I would usually punch walls. It was an afternoon double lesson and by now, I had a headache from not being able to eat or drink, I was tired, my throat was aching and being alone at that moment would never have been more welcome. I was ready for bed. She dramatically screwed my work up into a paper ball, aimed it at the bin and unfortunately missed. Another hour had been lost down the drain. Miss Tell continued, "As soon as you're done, let me know this time!" It was this class who more than others constantly asked me why I didn't speak; every lesson sometimes.

My new physical education teacher, in like manner, showed an even greater curiosity towards my silence than any others had done. I adored Miss Edley. She was small in height, rather bony with short blonde hair. She had an appealing look of beauty about her further pronounced by her prominent cheekbones. The very thwarting thing was that I knew I was able to speak to her and I felt comfortable in her presence. However, as things went, I never did speak to her because I was worried about the reactions it could have potentially provoked from others. It would strengthen the assumption that I only spoke to the people whom I had *'liked'* or chose to because I was too stubborn to act any differently. I did on the other hand speak several, simple shrill words to her when absent from the ear shot of others. For the vast majority of the year, our physical education lessons took part in the fitness suite; as much as I was captivated by a room of tread-mills, exercise bikes and countless other fitness machines, I dreaded using them. As it was hard for me to act non-verbally, running and other forms of physical exercises proved to be daunting in the face of others whom I felt uncomfortable around. Many of my lessons were the same. It was like a physical force pulling me back.

"What's the matter, Jess?" Miss Edley asked in her calm voice. I remained leaning stubbornly against the wall and merely looked up at her with a very small shrug.

"Why don't you come onto one of the machines?" I looked down at the floor, surveying the blue cushiony mats that sat before me. The many bright lights that burned overhead, the type that were scattered about in schools, only built up my headache. They made me feel sluggish, drowsy and made me long for nothing more than to be asleep back in my bed at home.

"Come on, Jess, it'll make you feel better." she rendered. *It certainly wouldn't,* I responded in my head. My head, throat and eyes ached and despite getting the fair usual amount of sleep, it did not stop me from feeling awfully tired. I always felt fatigued and tired whilst at school; it was another unfortunate symptom of Selective Mutism. My thinking and reacting were always very slow and my eyes felt like they were going to drop out of their eye lids. I simply hated everything around me. I felt more stubborn than any other feeling. School seemed exceptionally pointless, I could hardly ever concentrate, I learnt very little and it was only making things worse for me. I however took no responsibility over my own self. There was nothing I felt I could do about it.

Every break and lunch time, I would always meet Lucinda and her twin sister, Charlie, in a corner on the school grounds outside between the drama and art department. I always appreciated the fresh air more than I usually would have done after lessons; I loved fresh air and the cool breeze. We were always joined by a group of girls a couple of years below us. They were what students at my school referred to as 'Goth's' and 'Hippies.' I couldn't have possibly found a group of people who appealed to me any less. I must have looked very odd alongside them; too often, I would see people whom I had known from outside of school and they would catch my eye and smirk because of the people they would see me hanging around with. I couldn't blame them. There must have been about seven of us at the most and we always sat in that very same corner. The interests of subject were always rock bands, celebrities and anything of the sort which did not interest me. It bored me senseless … Still, if it wasn't Lucinda and Charlie I stuck with at school, it was nobody. I didn't mind though. It didn't matter what kind of people they were but that didn't stop the small minded people throwing snide comments our way just because they didn't approve of their stereotypes. To say the least, Lucinda and Charlie really were the finest of artists I had ever known, their work was perhaps up to professional standard; it really did fascinate me. They had been drawing ever since they could remember and they fell under the gifted and talented category at school.

It turned out, Tina, too, had left the school untimely. It had more of an impact on me than I had expected it to have had. Tina and I were very much alike; we had both had the same sense of humour, similar personalities, we both shared the same interests and I enjoyed her company more than anybody else's at school. She just didn't see it properly since she didn't know the Jess from the other world. She had always looked out for me and I did miss her. Now there was nobody left for me to speak to spontaneously. For some reason beyond my knowledge, Sharon had slowly stopped speaking to me too, so it had become difficult to speak to her spontaneously.

The contrast between my lives in and out of school was incredibly stark. Hour upon hour of school would pass without even a quiver of my lip, day after day, month after month … People would not indicate the feeblest of suspicion that I was even present, yet, it still felt as if every pair of eyes in the class were scrutinising me. It was a strange sensation. By the end of the school day, my throat would ache, I would get peculiar twitches on my eye-lids, I would almost always have a headache accompanied by that stomach sickness kind of feeling since I couldn't push myself to eat in front of others. That goes without mentioning the numb feeling which comes after anger which you cannot let out. On the way home, as I would approach my road, I would often see the faces of some of those familiar people.

"Hiya, Jess!", "Jess! Are you coming out later?" "Alright, Jess?" It often caught me in wonder. So I wasn't a ghost after all having lived through six hours in the belief that I was? There would be days when not a soul would have spoken to me in the whole six hours of school, yet as soon as I would get down my road, no fewer than three different people would speak to me in the time of about three minutes. It perplexed me at the least, making the whole situation seem unreal. I would usually smile in return to these greeting of friends and neighbours, or if my throat felt able enough, I could occasionally muster a friendly "Alright?" in spite of my voice being high and shrill. However well I would be capable of speech after this, my throat would still feel tight most usually until I had eaten that night. I had so many friends outside of school and knew so many people. It's what made school very difficult. I would then get changed and meet my friends in the park for more football. I would scream and shout as if to compensate for the hours of silence at school. I remember a time after school when I had been swinging on the swings with my cousin while I had been a bit hyperactive. The boy I was speaking to said, "Jess, you must get so many detentions at school for talking too much. I actually feel sorry for your teachers, you know." I nearly cracked two ribs laughing. Insomuch as this, a few of my friends too found out about my mutism at school. A close friend of mine, Daniel, once said to me, "My friend from judo class said you walk down the corridors by yourself every day and she said you *never ever* speak. Joe even said the same as well." I returned an awkward laugh and said, "Never speak? Honestly – can you imagine me of all people not speaking?" He chuckled.

"No," he said seriously, "but it's what they said."

"You work that one out then."

Often, there fell about few unfortunate times when the two different worlds interconnected. To what did I owe the pleasure of seeing Coleen at school? Coleen just so happened to be one of my closest friends and lived down the same road as I did. She knew me as well as anybody whom I was majorly comfortable around and it came as a shocker to her as well as anybody when she witnessed my behaviour at school. A friend of hers was close to my group of friends, and one lunch time, they came to sit with us in our usual hang-out area. My heart thundered as I saw them approach. *No. Not now. Please turn around ... walk the other way,* I thought desperately. Too late. They sat down, Coleen, immediately beside me. She must have assumed I would call out something enthusiastically like, "You OK, Coleen? How you doing?" as would have been expected of me. But no, I just about managed a feeble smile. Then I looked back down at the ground.

"You alright?" she said in a friendly tone. I merely smiled. I knew Coleen too well. I immediately knew she was under the impression that I was not speaking to her as if she had done something to upset me or something I did not approve of. The girls spoke amongst themselves for several minutes whilst I sat there in profound awkwardness. With my heart pounding very fast and my face heating up, I waited. Time passed. It could have been hours for as much as I knew. Coleen finally bade me an unceremonious goodbye which I returned with an unconvincing smile before they walked back towards the school building. I was overcome with relief. I just knew questions would be raised that evening after school. I quite frankly knew the first thing she was to say would be, "Aren't you speaking to me?"

"Of course I am," I replied reassuringly, "I'm just a bit quiet at school – as you can undoubtedly tell."

"I heard you were quiet but oh my *God!* I thought something was really wrong. I didn't think you, of all people, could be that quiet."

"Ha ha! You'd be amazed …!" I moved shiftily on the swing of which I sat. It always felt wrong, as if I was in the wrong. As much as I was aware of my Selective Mutism I could never shake off the feeling that everything I went through was entirely my fault. I was always overwhelmed with guilt in regards to my behaviour. Guilt was a big part of it.

In regards to my mother's opinion on my mutism, she had always assumed that I was 'Shy around big groups of people.' as she had put it, and believed that I was very quiet at school with no idea that I did not speak at all, as far as I was aware. Since I was so talkative elsewhere, she didn't seem to think very much of it. After all, I had always been like that. To everybody else, you naturally would put it down to shyness. Rowan had always been exactly the same as I had whilst at school. Other than that, we were opposites. He was simply an introvert and I was simply an extrovert. He didn't really have many friends, just a couple at school of whom I had known of. At home he was what I liked to refer to as an Xbox freak since he spent every second of his time on his games console when he wasn't eating or sleeping. He was a typical selectively mute, only feeling comfortable at home. It was so easy to label us as shy given the fact that there was a huge lack of awareness of it and who has heard of it? Nobody. If you are able to reply, you are just 'shy,' and end of case.

At the end of the year, I sat my GCSE exams the second time round after year ten. I had spent a substantial amount of time revising for them and going over notes … but it did not pay off very much. Altogether, I failed more subjects than I had taken. The reason being was of a result of the nerves and anxiety in the examination hall. My social phobia, as always, lingered. At such times, the world was a stage. There were about two hundred people occupying the room including part of many teachers and several examiners who were constantly analysing my behaviour. The pressure all built up sky high so I could not for the life of me concentrate properly. It was extremely nerve-wracking being watched and scrutinised by the examiners in a suspicious way.

I was always on the look-out for media about Selective Mutism and I had never had much luck until I discovered such publications by an author by the name of Torey Hayden who specialised in elective mutism (the term used for Selective Mutism up until the year of 1994). These books had me hooked. I was intrigued by them. They shaped my ambition to make people more aware of my condition. I could bet there were a great abundance of children and adults alike out there who, like I had been, unaware of their dreadful condition living every day of their lives at school as I had. I wished to share my first-hand knowledge and experiences with this condition with others in an attempt to help them overcome it. It meant everything to me. I wanted to do everything of my ability to make this disorder known so more sufferers could be helped.

Chapter Ten —The Symptoms –

As the years passed, I soon became aware of the other characteristics and symptoms that I possessed similar in other selectively mutes alike. A phenomenon which I highly appreciated was my introspectiveness. I believe it to have been a result of having paid so much attention to the ways in which people acted and performed around me in comparison to social interaction. Because I had not spoken, the only thing I could do was watch, listen, and observe human behaviour and to what was going on around me. As highly observant as I was I had an idea of what others were thinking and feeling in situations and why they did the things that they did. I suspect anybody introspective is susceptible to this, only I just had a lot of time to master mine. Thus I was very observational of my own feelings and thoughts and did a ridiculous amount of over-thinking on everything. I had a good sense of intuition, too. I merely trusted my gut-instinct and it was almost always correct. This was seemingly the root for my passion for psychology.

Naturally, I also became aware of my minor hyperthymic temperament and discovered my hypomania mood state. Hypomania is a mood state characterised by a persistent and euphoric or irritable mood with similar thoughts and behaviour to such state. The personality traits of this mood state that affected me were particularly having: increased energy and productivity, strong emotion-sensing, active and extroverted behaviours, being attention-loving, I was very expansive when it came to expressing myself and it had become a norm to have short sleeping patterns. Since my case hadn't been too extreme, I in fact saw it as a gift above anything else. Creative ideas would every so often attribute from it. What could possibly have been so bad about so often being in an exhilarated, extroverted and creative mood?

Perhaps as a result of my hypomania mood state, a creativity tendency stemmed within me. It had become a hobby of mine doing all things creative, like dancing, writing, and anything of the various sort. At any rate I knew I would always love dancing. I often expressed myself through dancing. Almost automatically, the huge weight that I had been carrying around on my shoulders for days would drop off in one longing, instantaneous moment. Hard-core dance music was my preference.

The changes were yet not all too positive; and there were countless, easily outweighing the positive changes ... My anxiety had without a doubt increased, reinforcing the Selective Mutism. In the same way, this made me worry more than I usually would have done but I discovered that keeping busy seemed a fine antidote for this. I also found myself being very indecisive. It was a near impossible task for me to choose between selections of any affair. I found it difficult answering and making phone calls at times as well. To my displeasure, I hardly ever had pleasant dreams amongst the dreams that I could remember. My dreams often included drowning, falling and being chased. I assumed this was due to the trapped feeling which constantly possessed me in my conscious hours.

There had only been one occasion where I had suffered with clinical depression ... and it had been most harrowing. There had come a time in which I had become overwhelmed with the taunts, the loneliness and my helplessness for it. I was trapped in a hole which was too deep to dig myself out of. Every single day consisted of the same routine: I would drag myself out of bed with great reluctance in my dark, cold room as my alarm sprang to life at exactly 07:00a.m each morning, followed by my struggles to leave home at the hand of my agoraphobia, soon to arrive at school for seven ever-lasting hours of scornful, ungainly, decisive silence. Thereafter, I would come home accompanied by a sharp headache, fatigue, an aching pain at the back of my dry throat along with a sickness feeling. I was never able to eat in front of anybody at school and by the time I would get home, I would be practically parched. I would then attack the fridge and almost as immediately as I stepped through the door an argument would break out (sometimes major) often over the fact that there was always very little food in the place. I would let out my rage of anger and the bitterness that had been building up all through the day whilst my mother would retaliate making me feel, if possible, a lot worse. My mother had a rather short temper and it was perhaps this which led me to my depression. Under such on-going circumstances I had become depressed. My life was going nowhere. Nothing was ever going to change … not with my life in the state that it was. Overwhelmed with helplessness, injustice and feeling rather drained and tired, one day I slept throughout the day over my mother's moans about me not being ill enough to take the day off of school. After a few days without eating and only sleeping, I had become very depressed. My mother called a doctor around to take a look at me to my massive disapproval but of course, I was unable to speak to her under any terms.

"Why are you not speaking? Cat got your tongue?" If only I was given a pound for every time I heard that. I looked at her stubbornly, hoping so hard that she would just leave. It had struck me as quite a wake-up-call to have had a doctor called into my home to examine my behaviour, and the very next day, I heaved myself out of my bed with every muscle in my body screaming in protest as my alarm interrupted yet another unpleasant dream.

I often worried about things with much intensity. This was perhaps one of the least welcome symptoms of all. My worries were usually completely unconventional, inconvenient, and respecting things which I needn't really have worried about at all. They were most specifically worries over feelings of anxiety and dread before a social situation. If we were told as a class that we were to give a presentation or such and such to the rest of the class, my heart would start racing, like a roaring fire, and I would worry relentlessly about it from then on in.

I was exceedingly indecisive. I couldn't bear to take the responsibility for something if there was another option involved which may have supported a better outcome. I had concluded that in behalf of my anxiety, I was most probably over thinking my options which made it nearly impossible to make a decision. Inasmuch as my indecisiveness, my life was more or less ruled by procrastination. I found myself fighting it day in and day out. I always thoroughly convinced myself I would do the thing which I had intended to do in the coming hours and then it would turn in to later, followed by … tomorrow … next week … next fortnight … next month … Of course, the thing I intended on doing rarely ever did happen. Taking this into account, my motto had become: *It's now or never.*

A daunting symptom was the constant feeling of being watched and looked at whenever I was out in public. Of course, I understood that nobody was really paying any attention to me whatsoever but I was equally certain of opinion that they were. I felt as if I were quite literally on stage as I walked down a main road. I was aware of every individual taking a glance at me as every car passed. This feeling wasn't unfamiliar. I had completely adjusted to it by now yet this hadn't made it any easier for me. I usually turned very moody at such times. My mood swings worked like a yoyo. The most common occurrence of this included the times when I had been mute for a long time. After an hour or two, I would start to feel drained accompanied by a very irritable, moody mood. I would then long for time by myself to recover.

Still further, it had always been very difficult for me to express my feelings. I almost always shrugged my shoulders in return to being asked how I felt or otherwise normally replied with, "I don't know." In actual fact, I never could string into any kind of words how I did in fact feel. I had encountered possibly every emotion possible throughout my life due to the reason of having Selective Mutism. As a matter of fact, I had often always felt a selection of emotions all at once. With the exception to writing on paper, it was difficult for me to express how I felt. It was very multidimensional and not to mention, complex. Generally, I would at times feel motivated, productive and inspired owing to my hyperthymic temperament coupled with my mass of frustration, anger and irritability over being unable to speak. I was further overwhelmed with injustice and indignation due to the ways I was always treated as well as the constant feeling of being paralysed, nervous, helpless and deprived. I was nearly always feeling upset and perplexed at the absurdity of such mixture of emotions and away from school I also felt provocative, joyous and free. In light of being away from my world at school, I had learnt to appreciate happiness; that's what I had found out throughout my life: at the expense of experiencing things at their worst you had come to appreciate things when they were at their best which you would usually have taken for granted.

In other respects I often experienced long outbursts of stubbornness. I was often unreasonably and perversely unyielding towards everything. The stubbornness would last for as long as I had come across something to cheer myself up with. I hardly listened to others and continually refused of what was asked of me. It was perhaps due to a lack of openness and the belief that I had unreasonably known better.

In the same way, a number of symptoms were physical. Often I experienced a shortness of breath and minor chest pains. It was nothing of great seriousness but it was meanwhile very inconvenient. I believed it to be a result of my heart pounding constantly. Another notable symptom, which appeared to be more outward than the others, was my body language. Although I tried my utmost to keep it as confident-looking as possible, my movement was rather restricted and demonstrated stiffness in such a way as though I wanted to make myself appear as obscure and unnoticeable as it were possible in order to avoid attention. Almost animal like at the worst times.

My diet and my eating habits had still always been remarkably poor. I had been forced to conclude that my extreme levels of anxiety had been the cause of this in turn making me too stubborn to try new foods. While there had been a reasonable handful of foods which I did eat, my diet had throughout my life been comprised of junk food. Junk food was the only food I had ever eaten. My diet pretty much consisted of whatever I wanted, whenever I wanted. Therefore, despite having always been of average weight, I was very small in height barely reaching five foot two. I was never able to eat in front of others, particularly at school. Besides, even if I had been able to do so, I rarely ever had an appetite during school hours in any instance. But by any means, I was however able to eat at restaurants or eat anywhere else in public if I had somebody I was comfortable with with me although it was difficult. It did feel awkward but I had always told myself the more I did something, the more it would improve - although this was not *always* the case with Selective Mutism.

Chapter Eleven –Sixth Form –

My first day of sixth form proved to be awful. During the past six weeks of the summer holidays, I almost drown in attention. I had been with my friends the whole time, I had been so confident and happy, and a minute never went by when I didn't speak. Then I went back to school. People never even looked at me. My friends from year eleven, Lucinda and Charlie, were in none of my lessons so they never spoke to me again. I had simply known this would happen beforehand, it had come as no surprise to me. I'm sure they were more than happy that they no longer had to awkwardly stick around with a mute; naturally, I could not blame them. I now had no friends at school.

I remember sitting in my new form room with my new form class and everybody seemed to sit away from me on the other side of the class room. It was so overwhelming and I cannot even begin to stress how frustrated and upset I was. I had felt like a ghost many times at school but this was just ridiculous. I even got marked absent. *Thank you.* That was the confirmation I needed to confirm that I was a ghost. I raised my hand timidly as my name was called, but this gesture went unnoticed by my teacher. Starting sixth form at Lea Valley at that moment had seemed like a big mistake. I was so eager to speak out about my Selective Mutism. I was aspired to do so. I had had the idea in my head for a while, but it was just doing it. I needed to tell somebody but there was nobody to tell. Apart from my mates, most of them being boys, there wasn't a person whom I felt I could open up to. The more time which had passed ever since I had found out that I had Selective Mutism, the more I began to accept it and the less embarrassed I was about it. Since beginning sixth form I felt I was ready to get it out in the open. Speaking out about the Selective Mutism, it sounds very petty, but when it dominates and controls your life, it's a huge deal. I knew I needed help, I knew it wouldn't pass as soon as I would leave school. For the first time in my life, I *wanted* help.

That first day of school was so hard. I came so close to having an emotional breakdown. I was firm of opinion now that I was literally living two different lives now. One in which I was an unpopular, ignored, disliked mute who never uttered a word all day and one in which I was a popular, energetic, bubbly teenager, who when it came to being talkative, would hear nothing against it. School was hard. I cannot express forcibly enough the intensity of the contradistinction between the both of my worlds. It was difficult being isolated in the common room alone with my racing thoughts, remaining separated from everybody else with their friends, throwing blank, questioning looks at me and derogatory comments whenever they felt like it leaving a horrible hole in my heart. I was seen as some sort of enigma to others. Sometimes I was near to certain of opinion that I *was* a ghost. It was perhaps the manner in which some people barged in to me along the corridors or perhaps the friends I had hung around with every day for the past few years walking past me as if I were not there or that they had never known me, determinedly avoiding my glance. Set side by side to being admired and beamed upon by my friends, the friends whom I laughed and spoke happily amongst, like I never had a care in the world.

After a few weeks of what I can only describe as psychological torture at school, I bunked a lesson and before long, bunking unfortunately became a norm. Shockingly, my attendance had been practically one hundred per cent throughout my whole school life and I had never done anything of the sort before. For me, school was social suicide and at home there was so much to do. Sometimes, some mates of mine would bunk school too and we would walk along the river skimming stones all afternoon. I needed such breaks like that.

When I was however attending school, every day for me was always the same. I had no friends and spent the duration of the day by myself. I had never become more aware of how sad life was when you did not have friends and I really had not been used to that. I had believed I had had some degree of a reputation at school over the holidays but apparently not. I was so, very lonely. I felt ashamed, suffocated, neglected, upset and unloved. It seemed to me as if everybody had hated me. Why was this happening to me? Why didn't even *one* person around me notice what was happening to me? I couldn't recall even a time when somebody asked me if I wanted to hang around with them nor sit with them in the common room. I would have asked somebody, placed in such situation, in the knowledge of what it had felt like. Even up until sixth form, I had always had the odd groups of girls talking about me. It was always,

"The loner girl with no friends" or sometimes, "That retarded girl." This was normal; it hardly provoked further feelings from me anymore.

Several of my teachers believed I was foreign from the assumptions that I didn't speak. There aren't even words I can pull out of my vocabulary to stress how frustrating that was to me. For some unknown reason, these teachers who expressed this view seemed to think I was Polish. I must have had some uncanny resemblance of a Polish person. I can recall a time when a supply teacher during an art lesson had taught us and somebody in the class claimed that I was German and that I had not understood what we were supposed to be doing. The teacher approached me and then spoke to me slowly using what looked like a simple form of sign language explaining the assignment. Despite all, I was a generally happy person and usually laughed along with jokes about myself, yet this time, I seemed to be the only student in the class who didn't find it amusing. This year, my Selective Mutism had never been worse. In other respects, there was also a factor of gender involved which made a difference when it came to whom I was able to speak to. Many selectively mutes seem to find it easier to speak to women than men, but for me, this was not the case. Being a tomboy, the vast majority of my mates were boys and I seemed to get along better with them than that I did with girls. In turn, I generally in most cases found it easier to speak to men than women. This seemed to apply so much so that I was more inhibited to speak to a male head teacher than for instance a female teacher assistant. Status under any other circumstance also applied when it came to how comfortable I felt speaking.

It seemed a primary statement that my education suffered under my Selective Mutism considerably and this was particularly the case with mathematics. My teachers assumptions that I 'refused' to speak to her were just insulting. Miss Steel always paused after she had called my name in the register at the beginning of every lesson, "Jessica for the *one hundredth* time, if you do not answer your name when I call the register I will not assist you with your work; you're rude to me so I'll be rude to you, that's how it is going to be around here. I will not tolerate your rudeness." I looked up at her with despair, overcome with dejection. I yearned to reply so severely, *Oh, I apologise, it's just I enjoy sitting at the back of every classroom of mine every single day being told off and being disliked because it provokes so much attention from you. Really – it's great having no friends and feeling depressed all of the time. Of course, one would only* choose *to act in such a way, would they not?*

"If you continue to ignore me I shall be informing your head of year. Is that understood?" *Yes please do. That way, you may actually come to some kind of genuine conclusion about my mutism.* It seemed to her that I had been, 'loving every minute of it.' I had had three different teachers of mathematics that year. I honestly could not specify one thing I had learnt in a year. At this point in the year, I was far beyond caring nonetheless. I was done with mathematics.

Howbeit, I was pleased that not all of my teachers were the same. My child development teacher was very pleasant towards me. I had always kept my head down and I got through so much work each lesson. Another shy, quiet girl sat next to me in this lesson and I enjoyed her company. In fact, I was certain of opinion that I was able to speak to Becky. I was too afraid to speak because if I spoke all of a sudden, people would think of me as an oppositional, controlling, stubborn mule. She spoke with a soft and discreet voice during lesson. She was one of the very few people who ever said hello to me; and she never failed to say it even one lesson. Her writing skills were not the strongest and once or twice she asked me to help her with her work because she was too shy to ask the teacher. *Bless her,* I thought. I was so keen to help her that my resistance to do so actually pained me. I loved helping people.

"It's OK, I understand. You can't talk." and then she smiled. I bowed my head in shame.

Psychology was perhaps the subject which I enjoyed the most. My psychology teacher, Mrs Edmonds, had also taught me mathematics for two years, and being articulate in psychology, she seemed able to comprehend the behaviour of my Selective Mutism better than any other teacher had done. She understood the fact that I knew the answer to a question she had asked me in defiance of shrugging my shoulders and it seemed she never drew any attention towards me in the face of the whole class since she had seemed to know how I had felt. Not much beat my love for Psychology. I was so hungry to learn everything about human behaviour.

In English class I was beyond everyone else. My English teacher was the cousin of my best friend from Chesterfield school, Shansel. She, too, knew of this knowledge and was rather fair to me in regards to my mutism. I always finished my work long before any other student in the class and all I had to do was put down my pen and stare at the whiteboard in front of me to symbolise that I had finished.

"Have you finished?" my teacher would ask almost automatically, surprised. Sometimes she read my work out to the class to provide them with inspiration, particularly my creative writing.

"I don't get it. What is she doing in our class if she can write like that?" a girl who sat at the desk to the left of me asked one lesson. My English teacher replied, "They've told her she has to be in this class because she is in the lower set for maths. I know – it's silly, isn't it?" She was not mistaken about that. I think this had been the second lowest of English sets in the year out of about seven classes. The girl continued, "How does she write like that when she doesn't even speak? She's finished, too, and I've only written one sentence." I stared out of the window, surveying the scenery bearing the thought that in just a few hours I would be out there playing football. It was a pleasant day. Football was undoubtedly one of the only things which kept me going throughout the school day. "Well, she pays attention, doesn't she?" she said smiling at me before continuing, "Do you read a lot?" I nodded tersely. "I can tell."

The secret to not losing myself up until this time was that I had simply always hoped for the best. Even during the times in which I lived through a somewhat form of clinical depression, I had no energy, no desire to do anything, and when life seemed but nothing of bleakness and despondency, there was still a glimmer of hope lingering somewhere within me. Perhaps one of the few advantages of anxiety was that you did tend to look forward to the good things that others usually took for granted; like playing football over the weekend and having a laugh with your friends or looking forward to the next time you were going away on a short break with Tracy's family over the holidays. Such things provided me with something to look forward to and kept me going. Together with this, maybe it was just thinking of the prospect of playing football and the company of friends that kept me going. In summary, it was these small things of the sort that gave me hope. Whenever I was upset, I would think about all of the good things coming up and the things I planned to do somewhere in the near future and it cheered me up. Positive thinking was certainly to be counted upon if I was going to beat this and tell somebody.

Chapter Twelve –The Revelation –

It was very sunny on Wednesday the twenty second of October. The skies had dawned a clear, brilliant blue above the school on an autumn mid-October day. My determination had doubled to tell somebody about my Selective Mutism. The thought that had motivated me, was that if I could do this, I, being the only individual in the knowledge of my condition, would be perhaps the first selectively mute in history to have told a teacher about having Selective Mutism; and that seemed a very near to impossible task to me. It was difficult carrying such a ponderous burden on my back when I yearned to release it so greatly. I had realised that *I* had to do this. *I* was the only one in control over my life. *I* was the only one who could change it. After all, doors did not open by themselves. I had a knack of looking so regretfully upon the doors that had closed that I missed the opportunities which lie beyond the doors that stood in front of me.

My history teacher, Mr Colligan, was a very good teacher. He struck me as the kind of individual of who was dedicated to teaching and who was always optimistic, happy and high spirited. He was from Liverpool, carrying a Liverpudlian accent and supported, in my opinion, the greatest football team. The previous year, he was one of the very few teachers who assisted me with my work during my history lessons as an assistant teacher.

I wanted to speak out about my Selective Mutism so immeasurably, but it was equally so difficult. It was like having the cure for cancer but being unable to tell anybody. It was most difficult having the knowledge of being the only person knowing of such a condition; for once in my life I wanted some help and acknowledgement. Another reason why I was inclined to speak out about it had something to do with the fact that help was never going to come my way. People were far too wrapped up in their own lives to realise there was a girl at school who was a complete mute. That was how ignorant people were towards Selective Mutism. I found it astonishing that I had to bring myself to attention. Procrastination practically ruled my life; it was always,

"I'll do it next time!" time upon time again and before I had known it, three years had expired. The words that ruled and dominated my mind were: *It's now or never*. That fact was pretty plain. As a result of my intense anxiety, when in a strong anxiety provoking situation one thing always played on my mind in a rhythm absent of my full awareness to keep me focused on what I was doing. Luckily, the *It's now or never* words stuck.

It was at the end of break time, minutes before the third lesson of the day when Mr Colligan was standing outside the canteen in conversation with some students. I took a very deep breath and vividly thought to myself *It's now or never.* As I approached him, he smiled and said hello. I had to reach the point where there was no turning back, and this was it. I cannot quite comprehend what possessed me to do this.

"Sir, can I speak to you after school?" I asked quietly and timidly. My heart raced rapidly. That had been perhaps the second time I had spoken a sentence since I had been back at school since starting sixth form.

"Yes, of course you can. You can speak to me now for five minutes if you like." I could barely even think straight – being scared was an understatement.

I nodded. I could not believe it was happening. *Was* it really happening? I was too scared to know. By now, the anxiety had kicked in dramatically and my heart raced like crazy. I half-expected my heart to spring out of my chest at any moment and I had started breathing out loud but by now owing to the fact that I was so scared, but by now, I had learnt to breathe discreetly at such times. Only somebody with Selective Mutism or intense anxiety could interpret how overwhelmingly terrifying this was. As we mounted the stairs some kid shouted out, "She doesn't speak English, sir!" He ignored this remark and asked, "What is it you want to speak to me about?"

"There's something I want to tell you."

"Oh, OK," he said smiling. I regret that I could not have been more specific, but I could hardly find the words. I remember the next moments like reality; the faces of the people who walked past us and the majority of directions that I can recall glancing in. As we approached the classroom, I started physically shaking, but I managed to hide it somewhat. I sat on the edge of a desk, and Mr Colligan sat on another about a metre opposite.

"So ... how can I help you?" he asked joyfully. Maybe this was not the right time. No. This definitely was not the right time to say such a thing; but then again there never was a right time for anything. I felt a jittery sensation in my stomach, squeezing my intestines with icy fear.

"I want to tell you why I don't speak ..." I said staring down on to the desk looking at my trembling fingers as if mesmerised by them. I could hear bird calls from the courtyard outside. The wind that intimidated the nearby trees was gentle.

"OK," he replied calmly. My hammering heartbeat filled the silence. Without even being aware of my doing so, I said it. "I have a disorder called Selective Mutism." I had said it in just one shallow breath and I could not have possibly said it any quieter. It was a trance-like sensation given my fear and anxiety. Jesus, was it even worth it. I thought of running out of the classroom.

"I'm sorry ..." he said, gesturing a speak-up sign raising his right hand behind his ear.

I should have known. I said it again. My fingers instinctively tightened the grip on the black jacket which I still held tightly in my shaking fingers.

"You have a DISORDER!"

His reaction saved me. The lack of serious tone in which he said it in destroyed all the tension in the room and I felt myself drifting back into reality again. I found the confidence to fix a steady gaze on him.

"Oh, OK. I see. And does your mum know about this? Has she taken you to get help?" he asked.

I shook my head. "Nobody knows."

"*Nobody knows?*" he asked sounding astonished. Again, I timidly shook my head.

"So I'm the only person who knows about it?"

I nodded. I had a huge lump at the back of my throat like what you get after you dry swallow a pill. Still, I refused to let the tears have their way. Questions then followed,

"Do you want your mum to know?" "Can I tell your year leader and inform Miss Field?" "I was wondering," he said, "because I saw you after school, while I was in the car, and you were speaking - I mean like really loudly, and I was like, *'is that Jess.'*" A vague smile spread across my face.

Mr Colligan seemed to have understood what I had told him and he handled the situation fairly well. He asked me questions regarding when I lost my voice and I told him about it. He asked me whether I wanted my mother to be told and I said I did. I think it was fair to say I was in minor shock during that whole episode. I was aware of what was going on but I was so scared, I just couldn't believe that it was really happening.

I cannot even begin to emphasise how happy I was when I left that classroom. For the first time in my life, I felt accomplished. I had actually achieved something worthwhile which I was inclined to believe I would never be able to do. *I had done it.* I strolled down the corridors like a king, opening the double doors I crossed two at a time because it made me feel like God. I felt like climbing to the top of the school building and shouting on the rooftops and for the first time in the whole six years I had been at that school I grinned broadly to myself. I just wanted to explode; I could have sung at the top of my voice whilst dancing down the corridors as the silent tears ran rapidly down my face glistening. There was something dancing inside me desperate to escape. The dirt finally felt washed away after everything I had carried throughout my long ordeal. I had never been so happy in all of my life. I was overwhelmed with accomplishment and audaciousness. I had fought so very hard that I had done it. I suppose it was quite the denouement of my life as far as Selective Mutism was involved. That was the day I had finally learnt to believe. One of the greatest pleasures in life is doing something people say you cannot do; especially something even *you* yourself convince yourself you cannot do. Now I was going to be getting help so it would get better.

The next day, Mr Colligan called me to his classroom during break time.

"Jess, you shocked me with what you told me yesterday, but you shocked me even more today after I read your essay. You know this isn't much better than the essays I wrote when I was your age? And I went to Oxford University." I enjoyed history, and admittedly, this essay was about seven pages long. It was even graded an A-plus which was the best grade I had ever been given for any piece of work in any subject before. After he had thanked me for telling him about my Selective Mutism, he asked me once more if I wanted my mother to know about this. I shook my head. I had every intention of my mother knowing, but after everything had sunken in overnight, I had realised I didn't want her to know. I had been in shock when I had said I did want her to know the previous day, yet, I still wanted her to be informed, but for a reason which seemed beyond my knowledge, I didn't want her to know. It seemed to be because I was afraid of her reaction beyond anything else.

In consequence, I was referred to the school counsellor called Mr Reid. I was given one session with him a week and willingly went to see him a few times a week at lunchtimes. Mr Reid was from Jamaica. He had thin, black plaits in his hair, brown, friendly eyes, and a retro dress sense. With a past of working for organisations such as Childline, caring for and fostering children along with his own, he was one who put others before himself. Naturally, I saw him as a father figure more than anything else. He seemed to be the only person who could look into my eyes and read the pain which nobody else could see. To me, he seemed to be one of the only people in my life who genuinely cared. There would be days at school when not a soul would bother speaking to me. I walked around with my head down; it was one of my lowest times. I spent most of the year communicating to him on a sheet of paper, yet, at the worst of times I had difficulty even picking up a pen to write with. Assumedly, this was because, like other selectively mutes, I had always found it difficult initiating and acting non-verbally in certain situations. Even the simplest gestures of pointing and nodding could illicit anxious feelings. I believe the people who you want to speak to the most are the people who it is the hardest to speak to. Whenever I was nervous or upset, my translation system would break down and my brain would freeze. I would think rigorously but I could not for the life of me string these thoughts into any kind of words. He discussed tips about my future with me, provided me with advice and tried his best to try to help me. Sometimes when he looked at me waiting for my reply to a question, I would stare into his eyes with such intensity that I half believed I would be able to answer him telepathically. At such times to my bewilderment he never did seem to know what I was trying to tell him. Any which way, he was a great emotional comfort to me. He had been the very first person who had ever stepped into my life to try to help me, session after session after session without a response from me. Most of the time, I just wanted him to give me a hug for the love I had so severely felt deprived of. I longed to feel security. His kind words and time towards me meant a lot.

I had no friends at school. More often than never, few odd people in my classes would say "Hi" to me every now and I would try to muster a smile in return, but no other student would approach me under any other circumstances. My subconscious would gape with shock in the event when they did. The lack of attention from others had impacted upon me. I would never leave for school without wearing make-up, and I had a mannerism for dressing in a sophisticated fashion. These things increased my confidence remarkably. Along with this, I was extremely self-conscious and very meticulous when it came to my appearance. I couldn't pass a mirror without having a quick glance. I can only summise that it was the social phobia. I started to take more pride in my appearance and dress in a certain way as others around me did in hope that I would fit in a little bit more. But of course, they didn't. The thought then dawned upon me, who was I to change the way I was, just to fit in with the crowd? If people did not accept me for whom I was, then they just simply did not matter.

I had grown bored sitting stone still in the common room for an hour and ten minutes altogether every day. It all seemed to depend on the expectation of those around me, and also, however happy I was which seemed to ease the anxiety a little. I more often than never went to speak to Mr Colligan in his classroom. Sometimes, it was a real struggle trying to pull the words out, and at other times, the words would just flow. I will never forget the time I spoke to him spontaneously. After a lesson, feeling in a rather pleasant mood, I walked in to his classroom and stood at the door.

"Want to chat?" he asked.

"Come in." I sat at the opposite side of the table to him, while he occupied himself with a bowl of soup. I looked out at the windows behind him, as if I were witnessing something of great fascination out there so I could escape his gaze. Silence crept among us.

"How was your weekend?" he asked.

"Wasn't bad." He nodded his head in an approving manner after tipping more soup into his mouth. I still gazed at the windows behind him.

"What did you do?"

"I went shopping … down Waltham Cross. And then on Sunday, I played football." A smile stretched across his face.

"Good," he said, smiling. He then pressed on about a story of his journey on the way to the school on his first day teaching there, about how students from the school deliberately pointed him in the wrong direction at Waltham Cross making him late on his first day.

"I wish I had remembered who those students were," he said, "I'd have given them a detention." We then broke into further conversation. And for the first time in the whole twelve years I had been at school, I spoke back spontaneously to a teacher, in other words I *initiated* conversation.

"Did you see the Liverpool game on Sunday?" I said. The conversation followed from there.

"So, why did you take GCSE history this year if you failed it last year?" he asked, still concentrating on his soup.

"They only let us choose from either history or drama." I said conversationally. It was true, I had little choice.

"I see. Drama is an interesting subject, why did you not choose that instead?"

"I can't even *speak!*" I snapped. I made my words firm, I would have loved to have studied drama, but sadly, my Selective Mutism meant otherwise. His laugh carried around the room. What was I to understand by the humour of what Mr Colligan found so hilariously funny about that statement. Then I understood the irony of what I had just said. I chuckled softly.

"Laugh!" He said grinning. I suppose that was rather funny.

"That is the funniest thing I've *ever* heard you say!" And he continued to laugh, abandoning his spoon into the now empty soup bowl after attacking the last of it. I had cracked a joke in just four words. I was rather chuffed with myself.

Nothing of any great consequence changed after the school had become aware of my Selective Mutism. I believe only some of my teachers were informed. To some extent, the teachers who did seem to know were more pleasant towards me now. Others who were not informed remained indifferent. I was still happy that I had spoken out about my Selective Mutism. Several more teachers in the world were aware of this condition; the chances were they would come across another person just like me in the future. As long as I had helped one other person, it would have been worth it. Mr Colligan had been the right person to tell. Who better to confide in about such thing than a teacher? I found it easier to speak to Mr Colligan than any other teacher. Since most of my friends had been boys I therefore felt I was more inclined to speak to a male teacher and felt less anxious in their presence.

Every now and then, to my delight, Mr Reid would interrupt my class and take me down for another session. Even though they were particularly awkward for me because I wasn't able to speak, I still enjoyed these sessions given the reassurance from another person. As the end of the year approached, we hadn't made too much progress in terms of my speech. I needed the knowledge that somebody cared along with the motivation it provided.

In the rear it had been a strange year. It had evidently been a thoroughly confusing one for me. I understood better than anybody else around me how severe it was being unable to speak in public. Yet, now, I was more than likely leaving the school for good going out in to the wide, terrible outdoors without my voice. I just walked out of the school for the last time with no last words from anybody. Did Mr Reid and Mr Colligan not understand the severity of my Selective Mutism? Or did they just simply expect me to arrive back at school the following year for my second year of sixth form? I before long found myself in another puzzling.

Chapter Thirteen – A New School –

I was not wrong in thinking my summer holidays were going to be satisfactory. I spent almost every single day going down to the football cages over the local park fifteen minutes down the road from where I lived. I was pleased to say I felt more comfortable here than I did even in my own home absent from my mother's count. These cages were the place to be. I met a lot of people there in the process and we would kick the ball around in the sun for hours. Some days, I would play there from around twelve o'clock in the afternoon up until eight o'clock in the evening. We would go up the road to get chips, fizzy drinks and ice-cream. I often brought along my younger cousin, Molly, who lived a few roads down from I. We were rather close, and with everybody else, shared some very delightful times. I loved football. It was something I played in order to let out my anger. It was social. It kept me fit.

I had also been in a relationship with one of the boys there at the time and I saw him on most days. Everybody who played there knew me. I came home some nights with a sore throat after having been shouting so much during the day. I was encouraged to shout and scream as often as I could because I believed my Selective Mutism would fade as a consequence. Yet, there was one 'problem' … Reeve. Reeve had been in my class at Lea Valley since year seven (for six years), and I don't believe he had ever heard me speak once during all of which time. He just so happened to live across the road from the field and was a regular at the cages. After five school years of sitting in the same classrooms as him, even sitting next to him and having never having opened my mouth around him, I never believed for a second I would be able to speak to him, let alone be myself and shout around him. It was very frustrating to begin with, only being able to speak seldom around him yet oddly satisfying at the same time. Look at the quiet girl now; the one who always sat the back of your classes, depressed; the one who had no friends; and the one who you thought was just nothing more than a shy, normal, girl. It took time, and to begin with, I was very quiet around him and I only spoke when he was at the other end of the cage. Answering his questions quietly was then to follow, and then eventually, I initiated conversation with him and in time, he turned out to an individual who I felt completely comfortable speaking round. I suppose the shaping treatment played its part in my progression of being able to speak to Reeve. I was ecstatic - after six years. I never thought it possible. Considering the Selective Mutism, it was simply miraculous. It's still hard to get my head around, thinking back at those times when he begged me to speak opposed to the times when he begged me to shut up - it was quite remarkable. I never imagined I would be capable of speaking to Reeve. Having been through six years of exhibiting mute behaviour round him stuck on my conscience was enough for me to lose all hope of initiating conversation with him at all. But I never did lose hope. Everybody treated me as a confident, bubbly person round him so it was easy to act that way. The differences between my behaviour at the cage and in the classroom were overwhelming. Football was certainly my most favourite thing in the world. Running down the field with the ball at a dancing dribble I was a bird soaring through the air. The anger that had been building up within me of the anger and despair driven from school was let out of me like a bullet from a gun when it came to blasting footballs. It was an incomparable feeling. It seemed an important recognition admitting football really did save me. I was incredibly grateful that a passion for football had been thrust upon me at a young age. I realised it would be wise to leave Lea Valley to attend Oasis Academy, Hadley, which until I had started attending had been called Albany School. It was rather an old school which my grandmother had attended back in her days. I found old school buildings interesting; it began in my childhood when I read a book about a haunted school. Ironically, and perhaps to my betterment, Reeve started Oasis Academy School too. Starting a new school seemed the most prudent thing to do; I believed it would make my Selective Mutism change for the better. Given the fact that people would be under the impression that I would speak normally and given the advantage of being around friends I felt comfortable speaking amongst, it seemed a very reasonable thing to do. Going to reception during the summer holidays was a challenge for me. I was certainly very apprehensive about it. My friends however came along which made it a lot easier. It took a while to reserve my place and I didn't officially get in until the first day of school. My close friends who lived down my road, Daniel and Mitchell, attended the school too and having friends with me at school who I had known for so many years improved the condition drastically. The head teacher, Mrs Dawson, was the first person who spoke to me after the receptionist. Mrs Dawson bore a similar resemblance to my old head teacher in ways; she had sandy blonde hair and wore a smart black suit. After a short conversation with her, she asked, "So, what's the reason you moved from Lea Valley?"

It had not even occurred to me to improvise on such questions beforehand. *I wonder what Reeve said,* I thought. I wanted to inform her of my condition, but the words were just not there. Even if they had been, I was unable to translate them into words. My heart once again raced out of control and I got shaky. I thought of a reply rapidly.

"It's closer to home, I have friends here and ... and I wanted a change of scene." I said this in one deep tone and once again with little enthusiasm in my voice. My voice shook considerably. She seemed to accept this and we discussed the options for courses for several moments before she walked me into the canteen to join the rest of the sixth formers in an assembly for the sixth form year. Somewhere near a hundred heads turned to look at the new face as I entered the room. I avoided eye contact with everybody and Mrs Dawson showed me to a spare seat. As I sat there listening to my heart thud hard against my ribs, I discreetly looked around scanning the room searching for any sign of my friends. I spotted Sid behind me; I had hung around with him a few times during the summer. That made me feel somewhat better. But, what that assembly was about, I do not know. Too many euphoric thoughts rushed through my mind and I was just too excited about break time which was to follow in the next ten or so minutes. Adrenaline flooded through my chest when I pictured myself speaking in class and making new friends.

When break time did finally arrive, Daniel and his friend, Shane, were waiting for me outside the canteen as I followed the crowds out of the double doors. I could have flown. I found myself shouting over the crowds so they could hear me,

"HA HA! You got *lost!*" Daniel said in that immature voice which I had become only too accustomed to hearing over the years.

"How did I get lost? I had to wait over an hour to see Mrs Dawson, man."

"When you first walked in, we all thought you got lost *all ready.*"

"No, *Dan!* They made me wait at reception!"

As we got outside, Daniel, Shane and another boy and I sat at the front of the school and Reeve and his girlfriend came along. Fresh air had never tasted so good. The excitement was unbearable. The sights, sounds, new scents and an urge to run and dance and leap possessed me. For the first time in fourteen years I was speaking spontaneously at school! I was deliriously overjoyed; it felt like a caffeine buzz. We were having a conversation about going to the cages to play some football during our free lessons and Reeve and I kept on looking at each other in disbelief at the fact that I was speaking. Reeve was a very confident guy who always said what he was thinking, but never once did he embarrass me by mentioning anything about never hearing me speak at Lea Valley in front of the others. I respect him much for that.

Later that day, Mr Buttle came into the sixth form common room and with Daniel, Shane, and Reeve by my side I approached him.

"Hello," he said joyfully and I returned a grin. Mr Buttle was a very friendly individual. He was popular amongst the school and a well-respected man.

"Am I able to take AS levels this year?" I asked, in my normal voice. No deep tone was pronounced yet my voice was still noticeably shaky.

"Depends on your results -"

"Do you want to see them?" I interrupted, in a loud tone which caught me by surprise.

"Yes, please." I restlessly fumbled for my folder in my bag, excitement bulging inside me, which contained my rather average qualifications. He took them politely and studied them for a few moments. I remember taking a glance beside me at Reeve. He smiled.

"Yes, they're fine; you will be able to take AS levels this year ..."

Thereafter my encounter with Mr Buttle I was shown to my tutorial class, my registration group. For the first time in many years, the tutorial classes had been mixed up of each of the different year groups, and my tutorial happened to consist of predominantly lower school students - years seven, eight and nine with three sixth formers including myself. It took a while for me to be placed into a tutorial since I joined the school the day it had begun. As a result, Mrs Dawson took Daniel's friend, Shane, and I, to our new tutorial classes. We were walking across the school grounds; it was rather a pleasantly hot day. Odd shafts of sunlight spotted the playground as we walked towards the building.

"The classroom numbers in this school are difficult to find because they're spread out in all different corridors over the school. Silly, isn't it? But I'm sure it all made sense to them when they were building the school." she said as our shoes clonked in unison on the ground.

Before even realising it myself, I opened my mouth in front of the head teacher, "Yeah, it is. At Lea Valley, it's more simple - like down the English corridor you'll find EN1, EN2 and so on and then down the maths - MA1, MA2 -"

"Oh yes, I know. They will be like that in the new building."

"Yeah, it'll make it much easier, won't it?" I continued in an offhand sort of way.

I remember thinking, *that's it, my Selective Mutism has gone.* I felt a lump in my throat and tears prickled the corners of my eyes. I could have reduced to tears but once again, having fought hard, I held it in. My throat wasn't even tight. The excitement of this was profoundly unbearable. It felt *absolutely incredible*. This was the definition of the word *free.* I would have given the world for those back at Lea Valley to have witnessed it.

As I entered my tutorial class in the old science building, my teacher welcomed me in and pointed a desk out to me. We were given a task to do in groups of four to make the tallest tower out of paper and sellotape to stimulate socialisation skills within our groups. I was placed in a group consisting of two extremely shy year seven girls and a year seven boy. They all looked up at me with the authority as if I was a teacher. I must admit, I felt particularly sophisticated in my white shirt, black waist-coat, smart shorts, tights and shoes. I was usually only seen in football wear. Don't look at me, I have Selective Mutism, I thought to myself. But I decided that wasn't the right time to be reminding myself of such nonsense.

"Erm - so how are we gonna' do this?" I asked particularly quietly. I forced these words out with such a struggle. Initiating conversation was my weakest point of all. One of the girls shrugged her shoulders in a timid gesture. I knew exactly how they were feeling. I knew what to say and I physically could say it but I didn't. It felt so wrong to speak without being asked a question. I sat there rather nonplussed for what felt like several long moments surveying the paper that lay on the desk before me as if I were deep in thought over deciding what to do. I was usually reasonably social with younger children and I possessed strong leadership skills earned from playing so much football with younger children over the years. It was a moderately disconcerting situation. I was feeling physically confident, tolerably comfortable but yet the words had once again failed me. There was still *something else* stopping me. I had then realised that had the teacher not been in the room or if at least one of my friends had been present in the room, it would have changed everything. Having been mute thirteen years at school in the presence of a teacher and a classroom had made it an inhibition for my throat to close up in such presence. Why had I not forced myself to tell Mrs Dawson about my Selective Mutism before now? It was vital. She could have made special arrangements for me under my circumstances. I *would* have done. I *could* have done. I *should* have done. Only one with Selective Mutism could interpret the extent of the difficulty of this, but I believe I could have informed her. Frustration flooded through my body. I hated myself for it. I had known what to expect, why did I not say anything?! But again, dwelling over this would only exacerbate matters. Regardless, I realised there were more pressing matters at hand. What was I to say? I was able to speak if I fought my hardest to, but I didn't. I could speak.

I wanted to speak. But I just didn't. The teacher was preventing me from doing so. Fireworks were going off in my mind. In my mind, I had a vision of the transfixed look on the teacher's face at the fact he caught me speaking and the class freezing in shock. Of course, I understood that this was an absurd vision given that he expected me to speak anyhow. These kids were just like the ones I bossed around at the football cages after all. In different manner after having been unable to speak at all or out of turn for thirteen years at school, this proved it to be an inhibition of doing so whilst feeling comfortable. Soon enough the supply teacher came along. Thank God. She spoke to us about how we could make our tower tall. I sat there nodding at the right times, trying to locate my voice. Then, as soon as it had come, it had gone.

After tutorial, I had calmed down a relative amount; I wasn't as shaky as I had previously been. All I wanted to do was to see my friends. I needed to find my voice again. For a strange reason, I had been at Lea Valley for six years and already, this school felt more like home than Lea Valley had ever done. I had seen a lot of people who I hadn't seen since I had left primary school and I was generally more comfortable in this environment. Of course, the hardest thing in the face of all of this was having such great amount of different emotions all bubbling up inside me at one time.

We were given the rest of the day off since it had been mainly an induction day. During the days which followed, the school participated in a project which involved a group coming into the school and in which students participated in activities and played games. I heard from others that they selected students to stand up and talk about themselves in front of a lot of people and that they picked people at random. That was enough to discourage my hopes for attending it. I was not going to participate in that. Besides, it was an induction week; school hadn't actually started yet, had it? That night after school, although I never did diaries, I confided in my diary:

Dear Diary, Oh my goodness! Do you know what? I think my Selective Mutism has nearly deserted me! In all honesty! I cannot recall being this happy in my whole lifetime and I am SO overwhelmed. First and foremost, I get into Albany (really Oasis Academy, but I have always known it as Albany school) and then I speak to Reeve, Dan, Marco and Shane (- Will from The Inbetweeners as Dan and I joked) at lunch time spontaneously. And then I spoke to teachers and other students comfortably. Students were much friendlier here and I felt I had been given a very warm welcome indeed. If you think it couldn't possibly get any better, I get to study four AS levels of my choice after I had convinced myself I would only be able to study GCSE's again as a result of my rather average qualifications. Then, this guy in the room comes up to me and introduces himself afterwards, since I just cannot take my eyes off of him. He even gave me a tour around the first floor of the school and that made me feel a whole lot better. It was Dan in particular, as well as my other mates who had brought out the confidence in me. I've always been so talkative around them, they were here and everyone at school expected me to speak so it wasn't so difficult. Can you begin to imagine what my first day would have been like if I had stayed at Lea Valley! HA! So frickin' happy -. I don't know how long this happiness can last. How today could have possibly been better - I will never know.

After another football busy weekend, I started my new timetable on Monday afternoon. I had been ecstatic during my first few days of school at Oasis Academy. It genuinely was a very big deal for me after being manifested by the severest of Selective Mutism symptoms throughout my life. Having a passion for psychology, I chose to study psychology, sociology, English literature and also history for good measure. I was very much satisfied with the subjects I was pursuing.

English literature was my first lesson. We were studying war poetry to my distaste. The moment I stepped into that classroom, I could have sworn I was back at Lea Valley once again. The silence had defeated me once more. My throat went tight, my lips were sewn shut, and my throat closed up. Deep down, I had a feeling I wasn't going to be able to speak as much as I had liked to. It was simply an inhibition to lose my voice in a setting where there was a teacher, a class of students, and a classroom present; particularly with nobody I knew nor present in the room. I was distraught all lesson. I saw my English Literature teacher, Mrs Douglas, as a big authority figure just merely because she was a very clever woman. She spoke like a politician, her vocabulary and grammar were spot-on and she could speak for England. She was rather squat, with short, purple hair, glasses, and a posh dress sense. She was a very pleasant lady nonetheless. Unfortunately, I felt extremely uncomfortable in the room and only replied in small, quiet words which I was always asked to repeat. Aside from feeling distraught, I don't suppose I could say I was disappointed, I could reply which was more than I could do back at Lea Valley. I was grateful for that much at the least.

Weeks went by and I didn't particularly know what to make of my welfare at my new school. I cannot deny the fact that I was better off here than I had been at Lea Valley, but at the same time, I hated it just the same. Soon enough, I remember sitting in my sociology class for the first time on a rather murky day, which was also used as a religious education class. I found myself staring into space (nothing out the ordinary there) eyeing the posters pinned to the walls. *The Five Pillars of Islam.* That one seemed to catch my eye. I was suddenly taken back to that time to my religious Education class back at Lea Valley two years before. It had seemed a long time ago. Although I still could not speak spontaneously in class, I reflected on my life since then. From speaking out about my Selective Mutism, to speaking to the head teacher of my new school spontaneously and talking down the corridors freely.

Unfortunately, I found myself skipping school once again. I very much disliked it after a short while. At Lea Valley, everybody knew I never spoke so they just left me alone and I was never panic struck when it was my turn to read because I didn't have to. I coped with my anxiety by not speaking. At this school, however, I was constantly asked questions, asked to read and give presentations, and I used to lose sleep over these things. Like most selectively mutes when they grow older, I realised that it was more embarrassing not to speak than it was to speak. I could no longer deal with my anxiety by staying mute, and this brought on so much more anxiety and stress in consequence. As the teacher would be going around the room asking everybody to read, I would find myself sitting there shaking with my heart thudding against my chest and going over what I had to read in front of the class over and over again in my head until I was almost saying what I was going to say out loud. It caused a lot of worry and stress. That was why I skipped so much school. I was aware that I was lucky to be studying the four higher qualifications of my choice, and as for the subject I was most passionate about, psychology, this was the only place I was able to study it for about many miles due to the course requirements. For the pain, anxiety and stress it was causing me and being unable to concentrate properly, I didn't even think it was worth it.

Long afterwards, they didn't want me at the school any longer so told me they were kicking me out because my attendance wasn't good enough. It didn't come as too much of a shock, although it did upset me deeply. Maybe they would have let me stay if I had told them about my condition, but in all honesty, I was half glad to have been gone.

My mother and I had by all means never maintained a great relationship with each other. By reason of my Selective Mutism, I had always had a very bad temper which I could not control at times but nevertheless, my mother's temper was even shorter than mine. It had appeared to be my Selective Mutism that settled our differences. We pretty much had different personalities. Unfortunately, it was the kind of mother-daughter relationships where one didn't tell the other anything. Showing love verbally was just completely unnatural to the whole family. My mother and Rowan shared a much closer relationship than that of my mother's and mine.

Rowan and I hardly ever made conversation with one another. He would close himself in his room throughout the entire day playing on his Xbox console, watching television or using his laptop. He didn't seem even too comfortable talking to his two closest family members. The Selective Mutism, on his count, seemed to have affected him a lot more than it had affected me. He hadn't really taken the opportunity to pull out of it like I had. I had always spent all of my time after school in the park, on the streets and over friend's houses, aside from school, so I had developed a social temperament when away from school and worked on it from there. And by this point, he had become too familiar with his introverted behaviours for it to change. His mutism was very entrenched. He just wasn't a social person. It was a great shame. Rowan had always been most talkative, confident and cheerful around my mother and I while he had been a young child. Selective Mutism had soon made its victim extremely stubborn, withdrawn and socially awkward around us. I could no longer see the ghost of that joyous younger brother of mine still lingering in his eyes no matter how hard I looked. It just made me wonder where it all went wrong for him.

Analysing the gender differences between selectively mutes, I imagine it must have been considerably harder having Selective Mutism being a boy. Boys of course have a nature for playing rough and play fighting etc and if one of the boys got you into a head-lock for a laugh, I imagine that would be a pretty awkward situation for one with Selective Mutism to get out of.

My grandmother, who had been one of the very few people whom we had always been comfortable speaking to in the early years of my life, slowly over the years, became one of those who it had become harder to speak to despite still seeing her every week. I had always admired my grandmother throughout my whole life, she was kind and caring. I cannot comprehend why it had become harder speaking to her.

Another thing which had concerned me, and through experience I had noted in other selectively mute children too, was that we sufferers seemed to have difficulty speaking in front of others whom we usually could speak to in the presence of the sufferers parents (in most cases, the mother). There were people who I would usually speak volumes to without a problem, as it was when speaking to my mother, but when she, too, was present with these other people, it became difficult. I can only deduce that I had become accustomed to not speaking in front of my mother as a young child, almost as if I had been programmed not to be able to do so having been conditioned to be that way. It was very unnatural for my mother and I to speak of personal matters too. The only subjects of communication concerned matters such as what time we were going out or if somebody had invited us somewhere as a family.

At a future point in time, my family were still as close as ever with Tracy, Louise, and her younger brother, Aaron. I experienced many highlights of my life with them. They were the most high-spirited, cheerful and wonderful family anybody could know and it was a privilege having them in my life; they had projected so much optimism into me. I feel part of who I am, is because of them. I was able to speak spontaneously round them the vast majority of the time, although the same cannot be said while others were present - particularly

Louise and Aaron's father. It had always been more difficult to speak to him than it had been with any others who I had been mute round. I believe that additionally, another contributing factor as to why I found it harder to speak to select people seemed to be due to their height. I was more intimidated and felt more uncomfortable around very tall people and less as much so around shorter people in many situations. Louise and Aaron's father of course was very tall and I had assumed this to be the reason it was so different engaging in conversation around him. It was very deterring and defeating because in turn my mutism towards him prevented me from speaking spontaneously to the rest of the family too. This awful, obdurate side would just pop out of me like a Jack in the box on its own accord at its own content. There was quite simply something in an individual's presence making it either harder or easier speaking to them than others it so surely seemed. Accordingly, it was more or less a set of rules by which I could speak at a certain extent and at a certain level of comfort. They had experienced my mutism so many times in such situations that they had become accustomed to it. This was down-right frustrating. I always yearned to laugh along with them at their witty jokes.

That summer, Tracy, Louise, Aaron, my mother, Rowan, and I went abroad to Turkey for two weeks and I had had the time of my life! The best day was when we went to a very uncivilised Turkish village in the middle of nowhere and rid donkeys, lye in hammocks, and in my case, broke wooden swings hanging in the trees because I loved to swing so high. After, we held baby sea turtles in their natural environment and then jumped back in the jeep safari jeep in anticipation and up we went up the mountains with thousands of sparkling stars above us on the rocky roads. I can proudly mark that as one of the very best days of my life so far.

Chapter Fourteen – After the Selective Mutism–

After I had been thrown out of sixth form, I unintentionally ended up taking a gap year. All of which time was spent at home, unemployed, and absent from education by the hand of my Selective Mutism. I had no intention of doing so, I was just too indecisive to know what I wanted to do and too afraid to make a move in the outside world. I liked to refer to that year as 'making the most of my youth.' Other than playing football and writing, I spent a lot of time going out with my mates and binge drinking every week. I started smoking too. I was living gallivant. Tragically, my Selective Mutism sometimes showed itself even when I was blind drunk. I encountered a time when I had been drinking in my mate's back garden during the summer when his older sister had come along. Despite the presence of my mates who I felt most comfortable around, I still grew very uncomfortable. I had drunk so much that I had decided to take a bite from a proper piece of chicken for the first time in my life. I could feel the warmth running through my veins, my head swaying, convinced a garden spade on the window sill was a sword and I waddled down the garden like a penguin away with the fairies … yet around his sisters presence, I was quiet. Regardless, I loved to drink. The joyous, euphoric feeling that I knew, was undisputed. During the summer I usually went binge-drinking once or twice a week and on rare occasions, even more!

I had had one of the greatest summers of my life that year. My boyfriend, football friends, and I, went down to the Astroturf at Rangers FC nearly *every single* day. It was one of my favourite places. It was perhaps the scenery and some of the people there that made me admire it most.
Some weekends, I would help coach some of the younger boys on the AstroTurf. That AstroTurf was my place. I loved being the person who bossed everyone about, telling them where to dribble the balls, what to do, and refereeing the matches. It felt great being assertive when all I was used to doing was being mute and told what to do by others.
 I spent the other part of my time with another group of friends whom I had known through another friend. As a celebration I also used to play 'drunken football' with two of my closest football friends. We would bring bottles of

vodka to the cages, drink it down straight and then play football. We had the most tumultuous time. I was the keeper in goal. Defending the goal like a corpulent brick wall, I barely even conceded a single goal. I felt unstoppable.

I adopted a lot of changes into my life when I began to go out with my new boyfriend. He was originally from Azerbaijan and one of the most striking things about him was how ambitious and career driven he was. It was my very first serious relationship I had had with anybody before. He understood the nature of the condition quite deeply and helped me out a lot. I never smoked a cigarette or went binge drinking again and started becoming more productive with my time. Due to my Selective Mutism, I had always been extremely tenacious, stubborn, but in due course, this, too, had subsided to quite an extent. I had soon come to realise that it was better to listen to what other people had to say to me than to not take in to consideration what they had said because I had believed I had known better. Over and above, I also quit my moaning and complaining dramatically. I had lost some close mates over moaning so much, but I soon realised they were no mates of mine after abandoning me under such circumstances in the first place. These were the kind of mates who only dragged me down. As I grew older, I realised people were always going to be walking in and out of my life. They were just a mark on the map of my past. Only the real people stayed. My temper had also ceased in like manner. Things were better at home as well. My mother and I barely ever argued. And finally, I was less moody, bossy and my domination tendencies and OCD (obsessive compulsive disorder) had deserted me. However, my social phobia and agoraphobia still lingered. I nonetheless figured that they always would, they had almost programmed themselves on me after being active for over long periods of time. I could live with it contently after having adjusted to it. It was reasonable to say I had matured from then on in. I had learnt to tolerate my dislike toward others whom I had every reason to hate; I considered and assisted the people around me and I learned to think before I spoke. The anxiety was always there but I knew I just had to live with it and not let it get me down. There is just no point in living life being unhappy. I had always been an extrovert. I seemed to think I was cheerful, considerate, caring, humble, sensitive and humorous. These personality traits are said to be common among other selectively mutes.

My confidence, after this, became sky high. I began to go for things, feeling the fear and going ahead with it anyway. I visited Lea Valley once again two years after I had left and visited Mr Reid. I was very precarious about how it was going to go initially. The Selective Mutism was proverbial to him, I had been communicating to him via a piece of paper for a fair part of the year. So the feelings which came when I spoke spontaneously to him - words fail to describe it. Profound accomplishment. We spoke mainly of all that had happened in the last couple of years and I showed him the original printed version of my autobiography. If ever I had seen somebody completely speechless, it was Mr Reid then. Was he aware that his mouth was part gaping open in surprise? I was pleased to see how proud he looked.

Thereafter, I created a support group in which sixteen hundred and still counting Selective Mutism sufferers and parents of selectively mute children joined and got together, discussing and helping each other with their Selective Mutism issues. Each day, parents bombarded me with questions regarding Selective Mutism queries and questions which I very happily helped them out with. I felt wanted and needed. It was all for a good cause and it felt amazing. It made sense to turn all of the difficult and painful years I had suffered with Selective Mutism for into something positive. I had my whole life's experience living with the disorder. I researched it, and used information from what other parents had told me about their selectively mute children in order to find out even more about it and to discover how to prevent it from escalating further and getting better.

I was then made The Selective Mutism Group (SMG) International Coordinator for London. I took responsibility in distributing information to those who requested it, educating through conferences, and encouraging formation of area support groups and providing support for them. I was invited to the annual Selective Mutism Information Research Association SMIRA conference in Leicester and gave a speech about my experiences growing up with the Selective Mutism. It was very well received and certainly a good experience. I was also invited by Dr Steven Kurtz to speak on the 'Hear our Voices' panel at the annual conference in New York, but since they were unable to cover the travel expenses, I had to give the experience a miss.

Among all of the things that life means to me the most primary of all simply being happy. Being happy is in my opinion the best thing you could possibly hope for in life. Life isn't something we do; it's something that just happens while we're enjoying it. I was happy the majority of the time, and that was the only thing that mattered. Despite everything of my past it was generally all of the time I acted as a happy, joyous individual. There is simply no point in going through life dwelling on the things that make you more unfortunate or unable than others because it does not make any difference. You can either live your life being miserable or live your life being happy, because the amount of work in any instance is the same. Being happy also meant not looking back. I didn't approve of looking back at all. You just have to keep on going. I suppose I was, like others, just a rolling stone. Every human being is unique in their own way. I was unique for the reason of my Selective Mutism.

Postscript –

Throughout my journey, I was to discover many ways which contributed to helping treat Selective Mutism. I had become passionate about the understanding of the disorder I had spent my life suffering with. I understood it deeply and the only thing I had longed to do now, was to share my knowledge with others and to help other sufferers to beat this. My long term ambition is to become a Selective Mutism specialist; it would make me happiest and make everything that I had been through worthwhile. The only thing I want to do now is to help people.

I had discovered an interesting phenomenon at aged eighteen. I believed, that to an extent, Selective Mutism is nothing more than the childhood version of generalised social phobia. Many symptoms I had thought to have been of Selective Mutism in adolescents were not just symptoms of Selective Mutism, but also more commonly symptoms of generalised social phobia. Social phobia symptoms such as: fear of initiating conversation, fear of speaking to authority, difficulty making small talk, difficulty making eye contact, pounding heart etc are all significant symptoms in selectively mute children. Both disorders are so incredibly similar to a great extent. In fact, I would go as far as saying they are the exact same thing. The selectively mute adolescent would realise that it would be more embarrassing to stay mute than it would be for somebody to hear their voice. This is because sufferers of social phobia, more than anything, fear that they will act in ways that will embarrass or humiliate themselves and they try desperately to look as normal as others around them do. In turn, they speak to avoid embarrassment and humiliation and to look normal, but cannot initiate conversation, just like the majority of children with Selective Mutism. It seems almost every other symptom exhibited in social phobics is prevalent in children with Selective Mutism. Essentially, I am saying that Selective Mutism *is* social phobia. This is just up until the time when the child begins to speak *only* when they are asked a question, and then it is then known as social phobia to them since the only symptom differentiating the two disorders is the mutism. All selectively mutes, as social phobics do, have difficulty initiating conversation along with every other symptom that they both share. Other significant symptoms shared between both disorders are having difficulty acting non-verbally (such as musical or athletic performances), reading aloud in front of a class, speaking to adults or ordering food in a restaurant. Just like in children with Selective Mutism, the exposure to the feared social situation provokes anxiety which may be in a form of panic, freezing, having tantrums and shrinking from social situations, particularly with unknown people. Is this all Selective Mutism is, a form of childhood social phobia?

Such a way for improving this disorder includes treating the selectively mute as if they had always spoken. I have always believed forceful attempts to make the selectively mute speak are never productive in the view of the fact that this will just increase their anxiety levels even further and in turn reinforce the Selective Mutism. I can admit that when being treated as if I had always spoken, all pressure to speak was removed and depending on the situation, I would then find it somewhat easier to speak. As stressed before, it's all based on the expectation of speaking. If somebody treats the sufferer as though they have always spoken, then they will feel more comfortable doing so since they are aware of the expectation. However, in opposite manner, treating the selectively mute as if they cannot speak only aggravates the mutism for they begin to associate themselves with the false impression that they cannot speak. People would then give up trying to initiate conversation with them and they would adjust to being mute. This was the case with me when I had stopped speaking in year eleven of my school career making the prospect of speaking seem more difficult than ever.

Simultaneously, I also believe it to be important to keep eye contact with the selectively mute as minimal as possible. Too much eye contact can be threatening and often made me feel more anxious and nervous then, correspondingly, made it more difficult to speak. Eye contact in anxiety provoking settings had always proved to be very daunting and uneasy on my count. I could not shake off the false impression that anybody who was looking at me was getting some sort of negative impression of me. My eyes almost felt as though they were burning when somebody fixed a steady gaze onto me.

At the same time, it seemed to be judgemental individuals or individuals who had known me to be mute who had triggered it in most situations. Accordingly, if one of such individuals had heard me speak it would provoke an extravagant reaction from them making me feel more uncomfortable. I believe it wise to have no expectations for the selectively mute and to respond to their gestures and forms of non-verbal communication as if they are speaking. A strong reaction about the selectively mute not speaking would also reinforce the mutism. The child should not be allowed to get used to alternate forms of communication or else it would become entrenched.

I would also suggest against direct questions with a selectively mute. I think it would be more appropriate to say, "I wonder if ...", "It looks as though..." and "I imagine ..." It would be better to say things like, "Can you ..." other than, "Do it ..." etc. Pressurising or tricking the selectively mute into speaking would only make things worse, making the selectively mute see the other as a perpetrator, if anything. I believe it is all about supporting the selectively mute and giving them patience and time. They need therapy and lots of support from all people around them. Please, understand, that children *do not* 'grow out of this condition' and the longer it is left untreated, the more entrenched it becomes and it *will* affect the sufferer for the rest of their life.

Impressing on the selectively mute that being happy is very important. I think you should focus less on talking, and more on enjoying your life and having fun. You will come to realise that there is more to life than worrying about Selective Mutism, and there are still loads of ways to enjoy your life. Selective Mutism is something that should not be a barrier to enjoying life. Selectively mutes are exactly the same as anybody else, the only differing factor being they have much higher levels of anxiety. I think this is an important thing to reassure the selectively mute child with.

Supplementary to the other contributors which I believe to improve Selective Mutism, it seems moving schools is an incomparable solution. Along with a school of new teachers and new students whom have no knowledge of the history of the mutism it presents the opportunity for a new start and a clean slate. It is of everybody's expectations of you to speak which would make the selectively mute feel more comfortable.
Other forms of treatment have also been said to improve Selective Mutism. Drug treatments like antidepressants such as fluoxetine or Prozac have been proved to be productive by reducing

anxiety levels to usually speed up the process of therapy. I had always accredited drug treatments to be effectual to ease anxiety and in the long term improving Selective Mutism despite having never tried them; it was not the comprehension of putting drugs into my body but more of being afraid of going to the doctor to be prescribed of them during the days in which I were alone with my Selective Mutism. Drug treatment is very controversial among parents of children with Selective Mutism. Some will say it has worked wonders, while others claim that it has made things worse. The dosage and age of the child are important when considering medication.

A further technique for treatment is known to be stimulus fading. In a controlled environment the selectively mute would be amongst somebody whom they were comfortable communicating to and then other people would gradually be brought in to the room, all taking place in small steps. The sliding in technique is where a new person is brought slowly into the conversation and the selectively mute would carry on speaking in their presence. Another additional factor known to be successful treatment includes the selectively mute communicating directly towards another. For instance, via voice or video recordings, e-mail or instant messaging. This is called desensitisation. Likewise the shaping treatment is a technique slowly encouraging the selectively mute to speak. When shaping, non-verbal means of communication are used initially and then proceed on to making small sounds, whispering before finally speaking which are reinforced from each other. I imagine these treatments would have more of an appealing effect on young children. Naturally, since my Selective Mutism was known to be 'shyness' no such treatments had ever been tried on me except the shaping treatment which I inadvertently experienced myself in an uncontrolled environment.

Another circumstance in which I found improvements was laughing. When laughing or giggling, to me, it seemed the part of my brain responsible for the anxiety relaxed or calmed down and therefore decreased the anxiety, in turn, making it slightly easier to talk. This could perhaps be a technique used to facilitate speech in selectively mute children in an activity they could take joy in when participating. Since selectively mute children are very withdrawn and do not tend to smile in anxiety provoking situations, particularly usually at school, this may get them to smile more and feel happier in their environment making it more likely to render speech.

Selective Mutism has taught me many things: one of them learning to value friendship. This is because I've never had an awful lot of them. I have had a very small handful of close friends and a lot of whom I referred to as football friends. It was rather difficult for me to make friends in regards to my Selective Mutism so I never took anybody in my life for granted. I soon came to realise that apart from the truest of friends, people walk in and out of your life all of the time. There were reasons why some people didn't make it to your future.

I believe growing up for the majority of my life oblivious to my Selective Mutism exacerbated my case since it's no myth that the longer you have had Selective Mutism the harder it is to treat. It is always important that the selectively mute is treated at a young age because otherwise the mutism will reinforce itself. The sooner the child is diagnosed and treated, the greater chance they will have of recovering because it seems the longer they suffer, the more accustomed they are to becoming mute since their life style tends to organise itself around it. It is a *learned* behaviour and the longer it persists, the more entrenched it will become. Like in my case, the mutism engraved itself upon me after being thrust upon me after so many years.

Also, from my own observations of myself and learned knowledge of Selective Mutism, selectively mutes are only able to speak when and where they feel they are comfortable and relaxed. I have found that I am most comfortable when I am with my closest friends. The reason being is because I have once again become accustomed to speaking around them and I therefore automatically associate being able to speak around them. I find I am always able to speak very confidently around anybody as long as I'm within the company of my friends.

The *biggest* comfort for me was playing football. Football had always been something I was always passionate about for it had given me confidence to exercise my leadership skills and socialise. For me, I believe this helped improve my Selective Mutism with incredible significance. The leadership skills and confidence I gained were just undisputed. Too often, I had been sure that I had been rid of the Selective Mutism. Because I had been controlling when it came to encouraging others on the pitch, a lot of people had looked up to me, and for the first time in my life, listened to me. I would insist that parents of selectively mute children got their children interested in a particular sport – there are tons of advantages of it when considering a selectively mute child. Or else be it getting involved in a musical activity, or another activity involving a social aspect.

Most significantly, I have reason to believe that belief is the most important factor involved in trying to treat Selective Mutism. Although you cannot exactly explain this much to a child, it could perhaps appeal to an older child. As I always say, you are what you believe you are. This counted as a huge contributing factor for me. When you truly believe you can achieve something, it has a profound effect on your mental outlook because when you believe you can do something, you begin to look forward to doing it. I didn't concern and remind myself of all the times when I sat depressed, lonely, with no voice at school every time I was in another demanding setting in which I was expected to speak, I pictured myself shouting and bossing everybody about on the football pitch. That's how I knew I could do it. Powerful visualisation techniques can have a profound impact on tackling the anxiety issues.

It is of my opinion that Selective Mutism, in the majority of cases, may get better to an extent as the sufferer increases with age. They may find it more embarrassing to stay mute than to stand the sound of their voices whilst they're speaking to somebody. It's the *sound* of their voice that they are afraid of, not of what they might potentially say. As a result, they speak, even if they can still not initiate conversation most of the time.

I ambitiously attempt to spread the word of Selective Mutism since our knowledge of this condition, nationally, is very limited. The more teachers and professionals that have been taught about this disorder, the better. It would break my heart to hear that other young children with Selective Mutism are yet to go through what I've been through. Selective Mutism is not widely discussed so it is difficult to decipher whether or not the child is mute or just shy. I hope this will one day change. Even a lot of the people who do know about Selective Mutism do not understand the profundity and the severity of it. It isn't just about being unable to speak when you feel uncomfortable; there are numerous symptoms which affect your behaviour, your thoughts, your life-style, and almost everything. I suppose there are parts of it that others cannot fully understand because of its great complexity. Nobody had ever known about my Selective Mutism. It was just like a big, dirty secret. I was more or less afraid of it until I had learnt to accept the fact that it wasn't going to go away in a flash. I suppose acceptance is a big part of overcoming it.

Up until the year 1994, Selective Mutism had been known as Elective Mutism but had since been changed by reason that 'Elective' was defined as a refusal to speak while 'Selective' was considered to be a failure to speak. In ways, 'Selective' can still be seen as a refusal of speaking as though children only 'select' when and where they speak and whom they speak to. However, I have always been firm of opinion that it should be known as 'Situational Mutism' or 'Situational Anxiety Disorder' because the mutism occurs in only given situations and this rules out the impression of children being too oppositional and only 'selecting' to speak since it theft me of my voice. But more than anything, this disorder needs to be recognised as a disorder, instead of some sort of 'attention-deficit, defiant, oppositional *shyness*' like it all too commonly is.

My story demonstrates with great clarity the consequences of Selective Mutism being left untreated and what seemed like a life-time going through school labelled as being 'shy.' It goes to show how humanity only lives for itself; so much so that I went through twelve years of school in my own world of selective silence unperturbed by any diagnosis whatsoever. Why was nothing said? Why was nothing done? Why had I not been diagnosed? Why was I forced to bring myself to attention? It left a weight of wonder on me.

The following year brought on many changes within myself. The most significant of these changes was my huge increase in confidence, the realisation that nobody cared and learning not to worry about what they were thinking of me. The social phobia was now practically non-existent. The agoraphobia, too, dispersed. As did the social anxiety and the Selective Mutism - not a trace. It seemed to me it all just passed with age. When getting so wrapped up in something, you tend to forget about being afraid and of what people think of you. As an ex social phobia sufferer, the only thing that mattered to you in the world was how you come across to other people. It dominates your mind in a public setting. You feel you are constantly being scrutinised by all people, and usually, convinced they are thinking negatively of you. And so the anxiety had gone. Nevertheless, bad days could bring on some minor anxiety. I would never fall back into the deep, defeating, deadly silence and I could always speak whenever I wanted to, yet, I would still feel a certain reluctance to do so even though I was physically capable of doing so.

Another significant thing which had changed was my introspectiveness and I wasn't anywhere near as observant as I used to be. I remember being, all the way through school, very observant of my feelings and every small thing which was going on around me. This, I suspect, was owing to shutting the social part of my brain down. All I could therefore do was watch and learn from what others around me were doing. I suppose, when you consider the traits of a child with Autism, you could relate. I noticed every minor detail of everything as a sufferer of autism would since, although both conditions do very much vary in terms of diagnosis, both an autism and Selective Mutism sufferer shut the social part down. Had a classmate walked into the classroom, I would immediately notice the scar on their arm, the jewellery they were wearing or the colour of their socks. I would then wonder how they got the scar taking to consideration the sports they are known for playing, or why a boy is wearing pink and yellow Mr Blobby socks. I suppose this may perhaps be another reason why Selective Mutism is so often misdiagnosed as Autism. This was how my mind impulsively worked in this given environment. I hadn't liked thinking this way. So many different, pointless thoughts about over analysing things were almost torturous when you just wanted to relax and socialise. I had just wanted my mind to relax and get absorbed into the one thing I was supposed to be concentrating on in lesson. My mind just wandered. One moment the Science teacher would be discussing Bunsen Burners, and within moments, I would fall into a deep daydream over football or something of the sort which I would hopefully be doing after school. Then, I would snap out of it and miss half of what was being said by the teacher and the rest of the class about Bunsen Burners. Reminiscing, even though the introspectiveness had made me more intelligent, observing things less and having an uncanny ability to look further into things, being less introspective and observant was now my preference.

My fussiness with food and my eating habits improved majorly too. I was now eating breakfast, lunch, and dinner; three square meals a day. I would now eat a very wide range of foods without reluctance. I would eat many forms of chicken and meat, most vegetables, nearly all forms of carbohydrates, and many other types of food groups. It took me a very long while to try new foods, but eventually, I got there. Admittedly, I ate loads more processed and junk foods than I would like to admit. When considering the very limited number of different foods I would eat as a child, I think it turned out rather well. Being very calcium deficit, I forced myself to try a glass of milk at eighteen years old for the very first time since I had been a baby. After that, I was drinking two pints of milk every day to compensate for my life's worth of calcium deficiency.

Always having had ambitions, despite my reluctance, I decided to begin college to study Psychology. Initially, having been away from education for two years, I was curious and anxious as to how I would behave in the classroom.

I went to college at The College of Haringey and North East London situated in Tottenham. Tottenham, renown for the riots in 2011 which were caused by the death of a man innocently shot by the Old Bill, was a very rough and rundown area. I didn't mind the journey either. An hour on the bus every morning and late afternoon blaring up my hard-core dance and Clubland music through my Ipod was class. It relaxed my mind and pumped some euphoria through my body.

All through my interview a few weeks before I had begun college, I was my confident, social self. I thoroughly loved my tutor and my main lecturer. Jean was one of the most approachable, friendly, and helpful people I had ever met. She was very easy to speak to and I didn't feel the least bit anxious in her presence. My lecturer, Luke, was, as well as our lecturer, a psychotherapist, my dream future job. The moment I was introduced to him, I had sensed some knowing ability about him. Throughout the interview, I spoke fluently and confidently about my circumstances and ambitions.

"You see," says Luke, "we are currently having doubts about taking you onto the course in the case that your attendance slips again and you are there forth taken off of the course. How do we know this isn't going to happen again on this course like it did at your last sixth form?" He asks intelligently.

"Well, this is my last chance, isn't it? I regretted it so much last time. I should presently be at Uni at the moment. I'm not going to let that happen again." Both Jean and Luke nodded agreeably. After a short discussion between them both outside, they were pleased to inform me that they would be taking me onto the course. Goodness. I had never been so excited in my life. For two years, I was convinced I wouldn't be allowed to study Psychology since I hadn't gained a B or at least a C, even, in Mathematics. No college in London would accept me. An exception had been made given my 'strong desire' to become a psychotherapist or Selective Mutism specialist. The excitement and determination flooding through my body ... I just wanted to tell everyone in the world! I was going to be studying a subject which I was profoundly fond of, at college! A fresh, new start. Two years since the Selective Mutism had last kicked in with any significance at sixth form. I was going to be my normal, confident, talkative self at college. I could not wait. It was a great big deal for me. I was very talkative at the interview, speaking very spontaneously, and I *knew* everything would work out so well.

Having travelled a way away from Enfield, I arrived at college first that induction day. Whilst sitting outside smoking a cigarette, Luke passed on his way into the building. We had a short conversation over if I was looking forward to the first day etc, and being my genuine self, I responded confidently that I was. I was buzzing sitting there. Excited isn't the word! Jesus, I was so happy because, in my heart, I knew for the first time in nineteen years in an educational setting, I was going to be my real self. I had been preparing for this for two years, everything I had learnt had been leading up to this very first day so, the last thing I had wanted to happen, was for me to go downhill again.

Eventually, we were lead to our classroom with the rest of the class. I happily sat down eager to strike up a conversation with the next person who sat down at the table. I then felt a stab of pain through the heart when I looked up to acknowledge who was pulling the chair from underneath the table to sit down. A literal stab of pain. It was only the lady who I had hung around with for years at school. Charlie. No way! My throat tightened immediately. My heart rate sped up so fast. How I hated old inhibitions! Then I knew that was it. I was ready to cry. I just wanted to leave the room. What was she doing studying Psychology, anyhow? She was a genius at Art as was her twin sister, Lucinda. Really, it was just incredulous. Why her, of all people? I had always had an irrational greater difficulty speaking to her than I had done with other folks back at school. *There is always* something! I thought angrily inside my head. I fought so hard. I just wanted to speak.

"Hi, Jess." she said happily, the expression of shock, too, evident on her face. I managed a feeble smile. I just found it amazing how fast one can go from completely confident to mute in a split second. It all comes down to old inhibitions. I was almost programmed to act in such way in the face of people who I have a history of mutism with. The first introductory lesson, if anything, was very awkward since Charlotte had sat opposite me at the table. It seemed to drag on for ages. It was life at Lea Valley all over again. Things had been looking so good, too. Luke and our other teacher of Psychology and Sociology, Denise, were at the front speaking the aspects of the course through. I could see Luke steeling glances at me from the corner of my eye every now and then. I knew what he had probably been thinking. *Gosh, she isn't going to be able to manage through the course. There are too many presentations and social aspects to the course.* This was what he had stressed at the interview; where the doubts for taking me onto the course were arising from. The thought certainly didn't help matters. Soon enough, the lesson had ended, and by the end of it, I was in a foul mood, feeling very stubborn, and just didn't want to speak to anybody in the class amongst the twenty odd people it was made up of. Because I was in no mood to smile, I couldn't have come across as a very approachable person and so nobody approached me. It was utterly depressing.

By the following and last (thank goodness) lesson after lunch, I had tears in my eyes. I had hyped myself up so much about speaking confidently and having had sky high expectations of it working out well, and in the situation where I hadn't experienced being properly mute for two years, it was just such a hard time. I came home that night and just got into bed and slept because it had been so emotionally draining for me. And I could never usually sleep during the day. But once I had woken up, realising it had been only the first day, I still saw hope for the next day on the following Monday. Monday, too, proved to have been pretty much the same story. I was ready to leave, although there was always a big ray of hope accompanied with this feeling. I always thought I could just go into college the next day and have a breakthrough. Day after day after day. But it just didn't happen. The only thing which had kept me staying and not leaving was just the fact that I could go on and finish the course and go onto University which was the only reason why I had decided on going to college in the first place. So given this reason, I forced myself despite the protest in my mind, to stay on, despite the same thing having happen in the last place of education. I had come to the conclusion that studying just wasn't for me given the circumstances.

The course I was studying was an Access to Psychology course which was comprised of units of Psychology of course, Sociology and Philosophy. There were mathematics lessons, too, for those of us who had failed to achieve a qualification previously, followed by an exam at the end of the year. I did absorb myself in the subject for the first couple of months, but there was just too much to learn and I still had great trouble getting my mind round all the aspects of the subject.

It was the same old story every college day of the week. Three days a week, including one half-day, were actually too much to deal with. My Philosophy lecturer, John, who was also aware of the circumstances, was keen to help me out. After consulting with him, we had devised some methods which could facilitate helping me to speak during classes. One of these methods included making some kind of gesture so I could indicate that I wanted him to call on me when I had known the answer to a question and felt the need to answer it. This, nonetheless, didn't work out since I also had difficulty making nonverbal gestures when in an anxiety provoking situation. He had assumed that the more I was communicating, even unspontaneously, in lesson, the more it would elicit genuine speech in any circumstance. Selective Mutism, being characterised as what it is, did not prove this to be the case. Over the years, I had found that most people, teachers in particular, had always expected speech around one person to render speech around most or all people. I have no regrets for informing the college and the tutors of my issues this time around. Being in the knowledge that they understood why I was pretty much mute put my mind at ease because I didn't keep on trying to act as if I was confident and the tutors went easier on me knowing not to pressure me into speaking. This, however, went two-fold. It did hinder things too because when people around you know you have issues with speaking, they're not going to expect you to speak, and expectation is what the Selective Mutism revolves round. I was friendly with the two mature women in the class who were in their forties. One of them in particular helped me out quite a bit, and there come times when I had communicated more than I did than others. There was a lot of group work involved in the course, and I found I felt less anxious and could communicate more on the table with the boys. As I had found it a valid point to note in a former chapter, as well as growing up as a tomboy, it seemed boys were less judgemental as girls were when expecting a verbal reaction. This is why I had had tended to mix with the males in the group more than I had done with the females. I think this was a factor, which over the years, had helped me to communicate further more than other factors.

During break and lunch times, as always, I had spent the remainder of the time by myself. The time was usually well spent in the library, and at other times, chilling outside with a much anticipated cigarette. College was very different from sixth form. Since we were more mature, we were given more freedom and were made to be more independent. This, if anything, had made it more difficult for me to mix with the other students in the class. As always, my attendance dramatically slipped. It was Oasis Academy sixth form all over again for me.

Just over half way into the college year (five months) when the deadlines for the assignments were approaching and the exams, it just suddenly got too much and I had decided to quit. It all turned into one big joke for me again. Why should I put myself through it all again? It had changed me - for the worst. My anxiety tendencies and inhibitions had come back full force. I was very unhappy, and going out less. Despite having managed over five months through the course, I just didn't feel I could do it anymore. I had plans for The Open University situated in London which was well-suited for me since the course was studied mostly at home and there were no entry requirements in order to get in. I suppose I learnt not to take things too seriously after that. When you do take things too seriously, it ends up hurting you.

After having applied for University to undertake Psychology, I began my novel and continued searching for a job. My local pub employed me as a barmaid temporarily and part time. The first day which pretty much consisted of five hours of training proved to be difficult for me. I felt I had to behave as decorous as it was possible because I would have considered it a delight to have worked there. I exhibited full force anxiety to begin with, but as the hours progressed, I started to enjoy it. Had I known exactly what I had been doing and not being afraid of making mistakes which you naturally would do the first time you attempted something new anyway, I'm sure the anxiety would have been left at bay. As a customer at the bar, never a time did I feel at all anxious, intimidated or unconfident. As always, I was very happy to strike up a conversation with anybody; I liked meeting new people. But when behind the bar, and being at the point of attention and service, I think I probably appeared a little bit 'shy' in everybody else's eyes.

"What can I get you?" I would ask, if anything, a bit too quietly. I would grab the glass, tilt it forty five degrees, pour the drink, put it on the counter, type it into the till, request the bill, and then bank the money. It was getting used to the till and knowing which glasses to use for each different drink and where all other drinks aside from beers exactly were. If I was confident in myself and knew exactly what I was doing, I'm sure I could have relaxed a bit more. Luckily, the barmaid who was teaching me had years of bar experience and was undoubtedly the best person for it. At the end of that first day, I felt I had a general grasp of exactly what I was doing. It was the social part I felt I had to work on next.

The next day behind the bar, I am pleased to admit I thoroughly enjoyed. The boyfriend was keeping me company at the bar most of the time, everybody I was serving I knew very well, and as a result, I appeared, and felt, very talkative and confident. I wasn't just standing there being told what to do anymore because I knew what to do. I was cleaning the counter, running outside to the beer garden to collect empty glasses and emptying ash trays, making the savouries and bottles more presentable, and anything else which would have kept me busy.

Given the chance, I would not have changed having Selective Mutism. It made me who I was. I feel I would have been more of a selfish, conventional, person showing less appreciation towards things if I had not suffered with it. Growing up and living with a disorder such as this has helped me to appreciate life for what it is. I didn't take life for granted. I no longer considered it a burden; I had learned to see it as a gift. It *was* a gift. It's the only way I could look at it. In disregard to the Selective Mutism, I lived the first quarter of my life enjoying lots of the remarkable things life has to offer. If I of all people can do normal things, any selectively mute can. Above all, I am immensely proud of myself for where I stand today after my journey with Selective Mutism. I am living proof that there is such a thing as hope and belief, and that anybody can turn their lives around if they believe they can. You can go through hell and come out sane and happy on the other side. I have never had any specific help for my Selective Mutism throughout the duration of my life – I had done it myself. Now, instead of feeling ashamed by my disorder as I always had done, I feel proud. It had made my life more thrilling and challenging. It is beyond me how I have got through my school years with Selective

Mutism without losing that spark of happiness. I cannot stress how grateful I am that it is now over.

I am glad I will never again be drifting in and out of my two worlds. I overcome Selective Mutism myself, so now, I can do anything.